Stephen

Defending Under Pressure: Managing Your Emotions at the Chessboard

MONGOOSE
Press

Publisher: Mongoose Press
1005 Boylston Street, Suite 324
Newton Highlands, MA 02461
info@mongoosepress.com
www.MongoosePress.com

ISBN: 978-1-936277-96-4

Distributed to the trade by National Book Network
custserv@nbnbooks.com, 800-462-6420
For all other sales inquiries please contact the Publisher.

Layout: Stanislav Makarov
Editor: Jorge Amador
Cover Design: Alex Krivenda
Printed in the United States of America

Table of Contents

Introduction   5

101 Training Positions   13

Index of Methods and Techniques   235

Acknowledgements   237

Introduction

At the 2015 U.S. Championship, Wesley So, a super-grandmaster ranked among the Top 10 in the world, was forfeited in Round 9 after repeated warnings to stop writing personal notes on his scoresheet. According to Chief Arbiter Tony Rich, the notes were *"words of personal encouragement and advice, the notes a player might write if he were nervous."* Among the self-help notes that Wesley wrote on his scoresheets are:

"Use your time; you have a lot of it"

"Sit down for the entire game. Never get up"

"Double check and triple check"

It's hard to imagine a player as strong as Wesley So needing such reminders to play his best. This example shows that all players, no matter how talented, can benefit from checklists and conscious reminders that help them to control their emotions or to find the right move or plan when they're under stress or not thinking clearly. These emotions become heightened when we're defending or feeling uncomfortable about our position (e.g., when facing a much higher-rated opponent).

These emotional reactions to danger are hard-wired. Early humans were exposed to the constant threat of being killed or injured by wild animals or other tribes. To improve the chances of survival, the fight-or-flight response evolved. It's an automatic response that allows you to react quickly without thinking. This reaction is triggered by emotions like fear, anxiety, and anger (e.g., when we get self-critical after making a poor move). When such emotions are triggered, the amygdala region of the brain automatically activates the fight-or-flight response. For example, in the position below I was Black during a 2013 FIDE-rated event at the Marshall Chess Club in New York City:

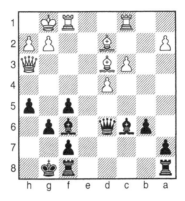

After thinking for what seemed like a long time (about five minutes), my opponent forcefully slammed his rook down and captured my pawn (1.♖xf5). Go ahead: Stare at that rook sitting on f5. You have to admit that it looks too dangerous to capture! Since this move caught me totally by surprise and he played it so confidently, I felt my heart rate jump significantly. My fight-or-flight reaction was fully activated! In these situations, there is a tendency to react impulsively in one of two ways: Either we "fight back" by capturing the rook at once (like smacking a bug that has landed on our arm), or we immediately take "flight" by deciding there is *"no way"* we're going to take the bait and capture the rook.

More often than not, the first reaction leads to big trouble, while the second reaction frequently leads to a missed opportunity to gain a big advantage. Purely on emotion, I rejected the capture of the rook and played the cautious 1...♗g7. Had I calmed down, it was not difficult to see that the rook sacrifice is completely unsound and gives Black a winning advantage. Try it yourself: After 1.♖xf5 gxf5 2.♕xf5, what is the simple refutation of White's sacrifice? The answer is 2...♖fe8 followed by 3...♖e6. Psychologist Daniel Goleman called these types of emotional reactions "amygdala hijack" in his 1995 book, *Emotional Intelligence: Why It Can Matter More Than IQ.*

The symptoms of amygdala hijack can be reduced by consciously activating our frontal cortex – the rational, logical part of our brain. This takes practice and persistence. The training exercises in this book, when solved using a timer to heighten your emotions, are designed to help you gain this practice. When your fight-or-flight response has been triggered during a game, your goal is to calm down and take control before analyzing the position. Remind yourself that what you're feeling is an automatic response, not necessarily the best or most logical one.

Don't try to judge or label the situation as "good" or "bad" when you're defending under pressure, were shocked by your opponent's move, or have just played a poor move. There are two main ways to manage amygdala hijack: Deep breathing and looking for multiple candidate moves instead of emotionally fixating on only one.

The four main signs of a heightened emotional state that can increase the likelihood of mistakes and blunders are:

- A significant change in our breathing (e.g., very fast or shallow breathing);
- A spike in our heart rate (usually we can tell when our pulse is racing);
- Feelings of anxiety or fear;
- Negative self-talk (e.g., "I'm so stupid. How could I have missed such an obvious pin?").

When we experience one or more of these emotional states during a tournament game, our mind starts to play tricks on us. In these situations, we need simple tools to help organize our thoughts and control the impact of those emotions. However, while these emotions can cloud our judgment and lead to mistakes and blunders, they play an essential role in our defensive success by "sounding the alarm" that we need to immediately activate our controlled thinking tools such as those discussed in this book. It's like a drunk driver switching over to auto-pilot to avoid an accident on a dangerous stretch of road. By the time you finish this book, your chess auto-pilot will be significantly upgraded from the version it was before.

Most players believe they're under-rated and that they just need to stop making "dumb mistakes" to boost their rating significantly. This belief is based in large part on the fact that we can find the best move much more quickly and accurately when we're not under stress (e.g., solving positions on our own at home) than during tournament games when we feel the pressure of the chess clock and the human opponent sitting across from us. When we're defending and our position is under pressure, the ability to manage our emotions and stay clear-headed is essential.

So instead of offering standard tactical puzzles to solve, this book is different. It's designed to provide practical advice on how to manage the emotional (e.g., fear and anxiety) and psychological (e.g., self-criticism) factors that can significantly increase our chances of blundering or of failing to find the correct plan.

Some quick background about me: I'm a lifetime 2100-level player (more than 300 tournament games at slow time controls with a rating above 2100) and achieved a peak regular USCF rating of 2192 (in 1988) and a peak FIDE rating of 2006 (in 2014). In 2016 I made another run at 2200 when I reached 2150. From 1991 to 2021 (as shown on the USCF website in the "Show Game Statistics" section), I won 40 classical (slow time control) tournament games against players rated above 2200 and drew 48. Those wins included four against international masters and several against FIDE masters.

Of relevance to the topic of this book, I'm a psychologist with a Ph.D. in behavioral science. For over 25 years I've worked as an executive coach for numerous business leaders in many industries, including several CEOs.

Business leaders are prone to some of the same emotional and psychological shortcomings as chessplayers. They sometimes make impulsive decisions. At other times they mentally "freeze up" and overlook crucial information. Often they (e.g., an Assistant Manager) are intimidated by an executive (e.g., a Senior Vice President) who outranks them, especially if that higher-level executive disagrees with their idea. This situation perfectly mirrors a tournament game where you (the "manager") are playing against a much higher-rated player (the "senior vice president"). In these situations, what counts is not just "what you know" (i.e., your skill level when you're not under stress), but how clearly you can think and respond under pressure. Therefore, all of the positions in this book are defensive in nature.

When under pressure, especially when having to defend for many moves, the tendency is to either play an impulsive move that only worsens our position (e.g., giving check with no follow-up move in mind, resulting in the checking piece being misplaced), or lashing out with a very aggressive but unsound move out of frustration and a desire to relieve the tension. Those two methods rarely work. So we need a wider repertoire of defensive methods to choose from in these situations.

Six defensive methods are covered in this book: *Prevention, Restraint, Only Move, Activity, Counter-Attack,* and *Transformation.* To help remember them during a tense game, they spell the acronym P-R-O-A-C-T. The first three (P-R-O) are cautious methods of defense, while the last three (A-C-T) are more aggressive approaches. So think of A-C-T as shorthand for "Action." While these methods are the foundation for the exercises in this book, I'll provide a lot of additional advice for managing your emotions within the solutions to these exercises.

Prevention

This is also known as "prophylaxis." Former world champion Anatoly Karpov is the primary example of a modern player whose games feature this approach. The idea is to eliminate or reduce the impact of your opponent's threats or future attacks. An example for Black is playing an early ...h7-h6 to prevent White's bishop from moving to g5 to pin your knight (with your queen on d8). Or moving the black g-pawn to g6 to prevent a white knight on g3 from entering the h5 and f5 squares. An example for White is to move the king to b1 after castling long. The king is more secure on b1 than on c1.

Resistance

This is a "bunker" approach where the defender aims to establish a solid position that can absorb a lot of pressure (examples: retreating a piece, creating a fortress of compact pieces and pawns, overprotection of a strong-point, etc.). For example, in the position below, Black can play ...f7-f5!. This prevents White from playing the aggressive f4-f5, limits the scope of White's dark-squared bishop, and establishes a defensive strongpoint on f5.

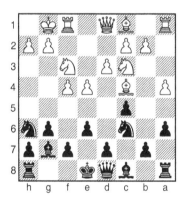

Only Move

When every possible move seems to be losing because of seemingly indefensible threats by your opponent, you are in an *"Only Move"* situation. The only thinking method that works in these cases is "2-part visualization": First, briefly visualize almost *every* legal move you can make. From that visualization you will quickly be able to reduce the list of potential candidate moves to one or two since most legal moves will obviously not meet the threat. For those remaining potential moves, slowly visualize the squares controlled by that pawn or piece from its new square.

For a perfect example of an "only move" situation and how to handle them, see Position T6 where Veselin Topalov, a world Top-5 player and former world champion, resigned instead of finding the two-move sequence that would have drawn the game! Notice in that position that clear visualization ("seeing" squares rather than calculating a sequence of moves) is the key to finding the solution.

Activity

Consider the following position in the Caro-Kann after the moves:

1.e4 c6 2.d4 d5 3.e5 ♗f5 4.♘f3 e6 5.♗e2 c5 6.♗e3 cxd4 7.♘xd4 ♘e7 8.0-0 ♘bc6 9.♗b5 a6 10.♗xc6+ bxc6 11.c4 ♕d7 12.♘c3. What is Black's best move?

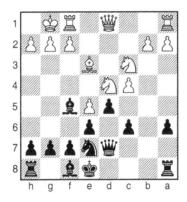

Best play is 12...dxc4 13.♘a4 ♘d5 14.♘xf5 exf5. What's going on here? It appears that Black is committing positional suicide by wrecking his pawn structure. However, appearances are deceiving since White has only a small advantage. Black has freed his position, has a strongpoint on d5 for his pieces, and has an open b-file to attack the b2-pawn. Had he not played 12...dxc4, he would have been slowly suffocated.

The principle behind the *Activity* method of defense is to look for moves that will free up our position at a small cost. The most common types of "costs" in these situations are allowing the opponent to capture an undefended pawn while we gain time to improve the position of our pieces, or accepting structural weaknesses (e.g., doubled pawns) in exchange for freeing our position from the opponent's pressure. Also, when there is no active plan available and we have no choice but to "hold the fort," maximizing the activity of our pieces remains an essential objective (see Position T76 for an example of how quickly our situation can go downhill if we fail to optimize the activity of our pieces).

Counter-Attack

This style of defense is characteristic of many openings. A good example is the King's Indian Defense, where White's massive queenside buildup is balanced by Black's pawn storm on the kingside. In this book we won't be covering counter-attacking opening systems. Instead, you'll find middle-game positions where preventive and restraining methods are not sufficient to save your position. This method consists of moves that contain immediate threats that force your opponent to take the time to address before getting on with their attack. For an example of counter-attacking in the middle-game, see my game against FIDE Master Ikrom Ibrohimov (Position T5).

Transformation

This method involves changing the dynamics of the position, usually with the sacrifice of a pawn, an exchange, or a piece for two pawns. Even if the sacrifice is not 100% sound, many players find it hard to switch gears from an attacking mindset to one that requires an evaluation of threats. They can't adjust to the change on the board, especially if they're in time pressure. So when your position is looking hopeless and your opponent is short of time, this type of sacrifice should be considered.

You will not be required to do deep calculation to solve the positions in this book, but you will need to apply a level-headed process to identify the best plan or move in each position. By the time you finish the 101 positions and absorb the practical thinking skills and self-management techniques they contain, you will notice a significant increase in your ability to find the best moves and plans while under pressure.

To simulate the pressure of an actual tournament game, I strongly recommend that you set each position up on your chessboard and use the timer on your mobile phone (see the guidelines for how much time to use in the introduction to the training positions). Solving these positions under time pressure will help get you out of your comfort zone, which is exactly where we are when we're defending under pressure in a real tournament game, especially when our opponent is rated much higher.

The training positions illustrate defensive techniques and methods for managing your emotions. The single most important defensive technique is to identify multiple candidate moves, instead of diving into the first move that captures your attention. So to get you into the habit of identifying multiple potential moves, seven of the first 10 positions offer you four alternative moves to choose from. For almost all of the remaining training positions, you'll need to generate your own list of potential moves, just like in a real game. In fact, identification of candidate moves is the single most important skill for defending when under pressure. Finding candidate moves is like converting a fill-in-the-blank test into multiple-choice format. For example, imagine two versions of the same test question:

Version 1: What is the capital of Alaska? Write your answer here:
_____

Version 2: What is the capital of Alaska?
a. Fairbanks
b. Juneau
c. Anchorage
d. Nome

If I gave this test to a random sample of 100 adults who went to elementary school in the United States, a much higher percentage of them would provide the correct answer in Version 2 than in Version 1. The reason is that many of them once knew the answer (e.g., when they learned the state capitals in school) but no longer remember. The list provides a "trigger" for their memory. The lesson here for defending under pressure is that your probability of success increases when you take the time to identify reasonable alternatives, instead of fixating on the first move that captures your attention. So instead of tunnel vision, you now have more moves to choose from, similar to a multiple-choice test. In fact, some chess puzzle books adopt the multiple-choice format. If you're like most chessplayers, you get a higher percentage of those puzzles correct compared to puzzles that offer no list of potential moves.

Consider your own experience. When you arrive home and go over a tournament game that you lost, do you often ask yourself, "How could I have played such a terrible move?" When we're not under pressure, the best moves often are totally obvious to us. The likelihood of making very bad moves drops considerably when we consider two or three moves instead of only one.

Among the 101 training positions, 85 are from my own games. All of these games are from USCF or FIDE events at slow time controls. There are absolutely no blitz or rapid games in this book! Most of my opponents were very strong players. Of the 85 positions from my games, 63 were against opponents rated over 2200, including several titled players (FIDE masters, international masters, and grandmasters). As a bonus, my only tournament game against Fabiano Caruana is included (see Position T77).

Now get to work on those training positions!

Training Positions

This section contains 101 training positions. They provide an opportunity for you to improve your ability to defend when under pressure and to manage your emotions. To heighten your emotions when solving these exercises, it's essential to use a timer. All mobile phones have one. For each position, set the timer based on your regular USCF tournament rating:

Under 1600	15 minutes
1600-1800	12 minutes
1800-2000	9 minutes
Above 2000	6 minutes

If you don't have a USCF rating or don't have a rough estimate of your tournament playing strength, I recommend that you use 10 minutes per position and then adjust the time up or down depending on how well you do on the first five positions.

When looking at training positions, our tendency is to quickly scan the board and find a move that looks promising. We then start digging into that move while disregarding potential alternatives. That approach works well with standard tactical puzzles that have clear-cut solutions or puzzles based on a "find the winning move" format. It also works well in blitz games.

Most of the training positions in this book are different. You will need to widen your perspective by identifying two or more candidate moves. Also, only a few of these solutions have a "winning" move. Most of them require you to find the best move to maintain equality or to achieve a slightly inferior position while avoiding a losing one.

So your assignment for these training positions is to:

- Ask yourself if the position appears to require a cautious method of defense (P-R-O: *Prevention, Restraint, Only Move*), or a more aggressive one (A-C-T: *Activity, Counter-Attack, Transformation*). This should take no more than 30 seconds. The purpose of this step is to establish the right frame of mind to start looking for candidate moves;

- Then, identify about three candidate moves instead of immediately focusing on the first one that captures your attention. This should take no more than about one minute since you are *not* analyzing any of the candidates at this stage: You are only creating a mental list of them;
- Only when you have the list should you analyze those candidate moves and pick the best one.

Don't skip the first step! Reminding yourself that there are several approaches to defending (P-R-O-A-C-T) will widen your perspective so that you can more clearly "see" potential candidate moves that you might overlook if you simply started scanning the board for potential moves.

In many of the training positions, there will be more than one "satisfactory" move. This will frustrate those readers looking for "find the winning move" puzzles. There are many other puzzle books that provide that type of practice. This book is all about improving your ability to quickly identify the best candidate moves when under pressure and then select the best one. In many of these positions the best move is the one that enables you to maintain equality. All of us lose many more games due to missed opportunities to equalize when we're under pressure than due to a failure to play a winning move.

So when solving these positions, the primary objective is to widen your perspective regarding what's happening on the board. If you find the best move for any of these positions but only considered that one move, you're missing a huge opportunity to improve your defensive skills. By forcing yourself to find about three candidate moves in every position, even if the first one that caught your attention proves to be the correct one, you're going to improve your defensive skills far more! Also, the thinking techniques in this book will indirectly hone your ability to spot the "clearly best" move even when you're not defending under pressure.

As you solve these positions, write down your candidate moves before choosing the best one. This is an essential training technique. It will force you to get into the habit of not focusing only on the first move that grabs your attention. Keep in mind that identifying candidate moves should not take more than 60 seconds in most positions. That's because all you're doing at this stage is looking for them, without starting to evaluate or analyze them.

T1: Black to Move

In a 2021 tournament game in Atlanta against a lower-rated player, it was my turn to move as Black in the position below. Black is a pawn up and has a winning position, but needs to find a few laser-like moves to refute White's dangerous-looking attack. Before reading further, take a moment to find the best move for Black. Evaluate these four alternatives and decide if each move is winning, losing, or equal:

A.   14...♔g7
B.   14...♕e7
C.   14...c4
D.   14...♕b6

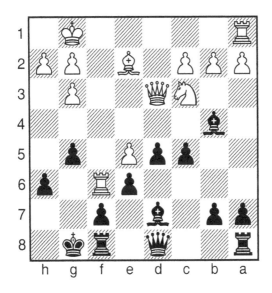

Discussion

After White played 14.♖f6, I immediately thought that my last move (13...c5) was a blunder because White now has the double threat of 15.♖xh6 threatening mate in one and 15.♖g6+ leading to perpetual check after 15... fxg6 16.♕xg6+. After quickly dismissing other moves (covered below), I told myself I have "no choice" but to play 14...♔g7 to prevent both threats. This is totally losing. For example: 15.♕f3 ♗e8 16.♖f1 c4 17.♕h5 and Black can't escape the mating attack.

I rejected 14...c4 (winning) because after 15.♕f3, it's too late to play 15...♔g7 due to 16.♕h5 with an immediate win. Also, I rejected 14...♕b6 (equal) because, after White plays 15.♔h1 to avoid the "cheapo" threat of ...c5-c4+ losing his queen, my queen seems to be totally out of play on the queenside.

Further, due to my heightened emotions, I immediately rejected 14... c4 15.♕f3 ♗e7, since after 16.♖xh6 my kingside appears to be falling apart. However, after 16.♖xh6 ♕b6+ 17.♔h1 ♕d4 18.♕h5 ♕xe5 Black is totally winning!

The lesson here is that defending when under pressure requires:

- A consideration of all reasonable candidate moves (i.e., not just purely defensive moves such as 14...♔g7, but counter-attacking ones like ...c5-c4 and ...♗b4-e7);
- Not assuming that a particular move *must* be played to defend the position (e.g., 14...♔g7);
- Consideration of all defensive methods instead of relying on a superficial "verbal" evaluation of the position (e.g., "I can't play 15...♗e7 because I'll lose the h-pawn and my king's protection will be destroyed").

T2: Black to Move

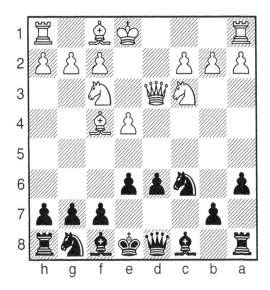

I had this position as Black against Joel Benjamin, a GM and former U.S. Champion. Evaluate each of the following alternatives and choose the best move:

A.   7...♘f6
B.   7...♗e7
C.   7...♕c7
D.   7...h6

Discussion

Alternatives A, B, and D are the best options. For example, after 7...♗e7 8.0-0-0 e5, the position is roughly equal. I played C, which gives White a large advantage. After 7...♕c7 8.0-0-0 ♘e5? 9.♘xe5 dxe5 10.♗xe5, I resigned since I can't capture the bishop due to the mate on d8.

What went wrong? After Joel played 7.♗f4, I panicked and thought that the only way to save my d-pawn was to get my knight on c6 to e5 where it would block White's dark-squared bishop from attacking my d6-pawn. This is a maneuver that occurs in similar positions in the Hedgehog system. I further assumed that the only way to put my knight on e5 was to play my queen to c7. So after Joel played 8.0-0-0, I quickly played 8...♘e5, which loses at once.

The lesson here: When we're under pressure and play a move (such as 7...♕c7) that is part of a planned multi-move defensive sequence, we need to stop after *each* move in the sequence to verify that the original plan still works. So when your pulse rate is up and you're feeling anxious about your position, that's the signal to follow these steps:

- Take deep breaths for at least 60 seconds before studying the position (step away from the board to do this);

- Find at least three candidate moves to consider, rather than assuming there is only one "must-play" move (e.g., 8...♘e5??). Since I told myself that I would play ...♘c6-e5 after ...♕c7, I wasted no time before playing that blunder!

- When visualizing each of those candidate moves, you must do a full "blunder check" by concretely analyzing all forcing tactics (i.e., captures, sacrifices, double attacks, checks, etc.) 2-3 moves deep that are available to your opponent. That's because 95% of blunders involve "immediate" oversights within a span of 1-3 moves;

- Understanding these steps is easy. Remembering to do them in the heat of the moment is hard. So, when you're taking those deep breaths, that is the time to remind yourself to do the second and third steps above when you return to the board. In fact, *anytime* during a tournament game when you feel a spike in your emotions or pulse rate, it's essential to hit the emotional "reset button" by doing 60 seconds of deep breathing!

T3: Black to Move

In 2003 I won the U.S. Amateur Championship for the Eastern Region. In this event, I was Black in the final round against Ian Prevost, a 2100 player who was in sole first place. I was a half-point behind. I noticed in prior rounds that he was playing very aggressive openings and winning with sharp attacks. With the championship on the line against such an aggressive player, my pulse was rising even before our game started! So when he played the Smith-Morra Gambit against me (1.e4 c5 2.d4 cxd4 3.c3), I declined by playing 3...♘f6. After the moves 1.e4 c5 2.d4 cxd4 3.c3 ♘f6 4.e5 ♘d5 5.cxd4 d6 6.♘f3 ♘c6 7.♗c4 ♘b6 8.♗b3 e6 9.0-0 ♗e7 10.♘c3, we reached this position:

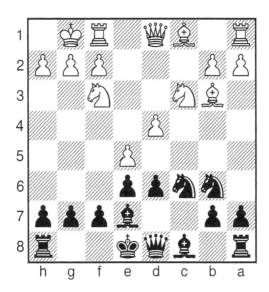

If you were playing this game instead of me, what move would you choose?

A. 10...dxe5
B. 10...d5
C. 10...0-0
D. 10...a6

Discussion

This is a trick question, since all of the moves are reasonable choices, though the move I played (10...d5) was objectively the weakest of the four. However, it's important to consider our emotions and our opponent's playing style when choosing our openings and moves that can alter the dynamics of the position (e.g., accepting versus declining the gambit pawn).

Based on my heightened emotions and my opponent's eagerness to attack, I made two level-headed decisions that helped me win this crucial game: First, I declined the gambit (3...♞f6), even though objectively speaking, the strongest move is to accept the gambit pawn. Second, I converted the game into a position resembling the French Defense by "wasting a tempo" to play ...d6-d5 after previously playing ...d7-d6. My objective was to close the position (e.g., by reducing the diagonal for his light-squared bishop and controlling the e4 square so his pieces couldn't use it for attacking purposes). Once I closed the position, he lost his bearings and I outplayed him positionally. Here's the rest of the game:

10...d5 11.♗c2 ♗d7 12.a3 a6 13.♕d3 ♞a7 14.♖e1 h6 15.b3 ♕c7 16.♗b2 0-0-0 17.♕e2 ♚b8 18.♗d3 ♖c8 19.♖ec1 ♕d8 20.♞d1 ♗b5 21.♞e3 ♕d7 22.♞d2 ♗xd3 23.♕xd3 ♖xc1+ 24.♖xc1 a5 25.♞b1 a4 26.b4 ♞bc8 27.g3 b5 28.♚f1 ♞b6 29.f4 ♞c4 30.♞xc4 dxc4 31.♕e4 ♕b7 32.♕xb7+ ♚xb7 33.♞c3 ♚c6 34.♖d1 ♖d8 35.♚e2 ♞c8 36.♚f3 ♞b6 37.♚e4 h5 38.♖f1 g6 39.♖f3 f5+ 40.♚e3 g5 41.♞e2 g4 42.♖f2 h4 43.gxh4 ♖h8 44.♖g2 ♖xh4 45.♖f2 ♖h3+ 46.♚d2 ♞d5 47.♗c3 ♗h4 48.♖g2 ♖d3+ **0-1**

The moral of this story is that you must take your emotional state into account, especially when playing Black. Objectively speaking, taking the gambit pawn on move 3 and not playing ...d6-d5 on move 10 would have been the "best" moves. However, with my heightened emotions and my opponent's attacking style, I played "weaker" moves that fit my own playing style while forcing my opponent out of his comfort zone into a maneuvering game. So while most of the exercises in this book shed light on how to handle pressure when defending, this position is a great example of how to *avoid* some types of pressure by changing the dynamics of the position via sound but "second-best" moves.

T4: Black to Move

My opponent in this game was Brandon Jacobson (rated 2350 at the time of this game and now a grandmaster). It was my turn to move as Black. Evaluate these four moves and choose the best one:

A. ...⧮dxd4
B. ...♝c8
C. ...fxe4
D. ...♝b7

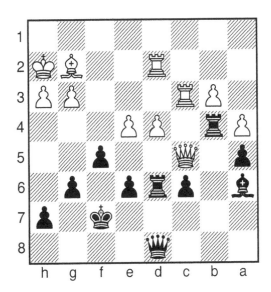

Discussion

The last three choices all give Black a roughly equal position. Instead, I played ...♖dxd4 (a big blunder). I was rated over 2100 at the time, so this type of blunder was inexcusable. So what triggered my mistake? At this point in the game, I had been defending for many moves and had used up a lot of energy. When we're low on energy and defending under pressure, we're more likely to see "phantom" threats (e.g., "if White plays e5, my rook can't defend the c6-pawn") and lash out impulsively to meet those threats.

In such situations, "forcing" moves such as captures feel safer than passive waiting moves because we assume that it slows down the opponent's pressure. Because the move is so forcing ("he has to recapture"), we often don't calculate an additional two or three moves ahead because we assume we can do that after the opponent recaptures. After the exchange of a pairs of rooks on d4, White played the simple ♕a7+, winning my bishop.

By focusing so heavily on the main point of contact between the two armies (the d4 square in this example), we can miss tactical shots on other parts of the board (e.g., ♕a7+). The other issue in this example is that by capturing the pawn on d4, I triggered a series of tactical moves, not just a simple recapture.

So the lesson here is: When you are tired and under pressure, do not take threats at face value. Also, do not initiate a tactical exchange without first looking at additional moves after your opponent takes back. Never tell yourself that *"He has to recapture. So instead of wasting time, I'll wait until after he recaptures to figure out my next move."*

T5: Black to Move

My opponent was Ikrom Ibrohimov, a FIDE master with a USCF rating of 2400. This game was played in a FIDE-rated event at the Marshall Chess Club in New York City in 2015. It was my turn to move as Black in this position:

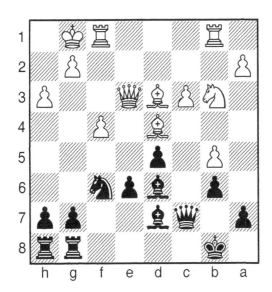

Evaluate these alternatives and select the best move:

A.   32...♖f8
B.   32...h5
C.   32...♖e8
D.   32...♞h5

Discussion

When facing a much higher-rated player (e.g., someone more than 300 points above you), some players have no anxiety at all because they assume they will lose and therefore have a relaxed attitude, while others have a lot of anxiety because the fear of getting "crushed" makes them very uncomfortable. Either state of mind makes it hard to play your best. In the position above, I had been defending for over two hours. Because of that (along with my opponent's high rating), I felt that his position was much better than mine. I thought he had threats on both sides of the board (e.g., g2-g4 on the kingside and a2-a4-a5 on the queenside with a vicious attack). So I told myself I can only deal with one threat at a time and played ...h7-h5. This is a losing move! Instead, ...♞h5 gives Black a fully equal position and the other two moves allow White only a slight edge.

When we've been defending for many moves against a higher-rated player, there is a natural tendency to either make an impulsive move (especially a capture as in Position T4) to relieve the pressure, or to play very passively and try to "hold" the position. In these situations we rarely look for counter-attacking moves. In this position, ...♞h5 begins a perfectly-timed *Counter-Attack* on the kingside. All six of Black's pieces are aiming in that direction! Also, there is an immediate threat to the f4-pawn. White can't play g2-g3 because Black counters with ...g7-g5!. Best play in this position is 32...♞h5! 33.♗e5 ♖f8 34.g3 g5! 35.♗xh8 gxf4 36.♕d4 ♞xg3 with an equal position.

The lesson here is that no matter what your opponent's rating is and how long you've been defending, you must actively look for counter-attacking ideas to complement more purely defensive moves. My ...h7-h5 push was a waste of precious time, allowing White to start an unstoppable attack with a2-a4-a5. I could have totally changed the flow of the game with ...♞h5. Keep in mind that most counter-attacking ideas don't require a huge amount of precise calculation. What's important is being on the lookout for those ideas and in most cases you will see the main themes fairly quickly.

T6: Black to Move

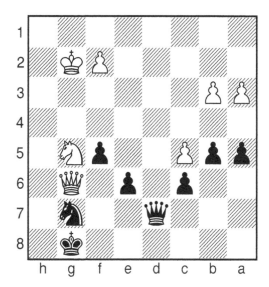

Black has been defending for many moves and the game has reached a critical position. What is Black's best move?

Discussion

This position is from Carlsen – Topalov, Linares 2007. In this position, Topalov resigned! The stress of defending for so long against the player who everyone knew was destined to be World Champion took its toll on Topalov.

When feeling discouraged and exhausted in a position that appears hopeless, it's essential to consider *every* reasonable legal move. Since White is threatening ♕h7+ followed by ♕h8+ and then ♕xg7 winning the knight, ...f5-f4 (for example) would not be a reasonable move for Black to consider. However, certainly most queen moves should be considered. One of those moves is ...♕d5+. So far, so good. White has to remove his king from check, so Black "lives" for at least a few more moves. With the queen sitting on d5, then visualize all of the squares it's connected to, including those currently blocked by pawns.

At this point the solution becomes visible. If Black plays ...♕d5+ followed by ...e6-e5, the queen is guarding the g8 square! So now White's intended ♕h7+ followed by ♕h8+ is met by ...♕g8, blocking the check and defending the knight on g7. This non-obvious defensive solution involving a "zigzag" queen maneuver is similar to the one I failed to find in the first position in this book.

This example shows that even world champions like Topalov who are under pressure can fail to solve positions that they could solve in their sleep if not for the pressure and stress. The solution is not that difficult to find *if* you consider every reasonable legal move and then clearly visualize *all* of the squares that piece "touches" from its new position. I was able to solve this position by applying this approach.

Do you have any doubt that Topalov would find the solution to this position in well under a minute if he came across it in a chess puzzle book? I have no doubt whatsoever. This is a powerful example of how we must rely on structured thinking techniques ("look at every legal move") in situations where we're walking a tightrope and need to find "only moves" to survive. In such cases, calm visualization (here, of the squares the black queen touches from d5) is often more important than calculation of variations.

T7: White to Move

In a FIDE-rated event at the Marshall Chess Club in 2013, I was White against 2400-rated FIDE Master Rawle Allicock. We reached this position with me to move:

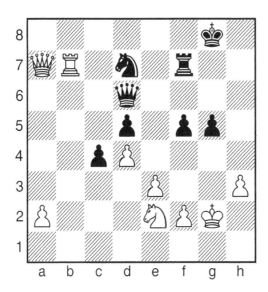

Evaluate the following alternatives and choose one. Also, determine which move is the *worst* one (and why).

    A.   54.♕a5
    B.   54.f4
    C.   54.♕a8+
    D.   54.♖b5

Discussion

At this point in the game, I was down to about 15 minutes on the clock and my opponent had about 20 minutes. That time pressure, along with Black's initiative on the kingside, made me nervous. So my emotional reaction was to look for a way to directly blunt his pressure. I played 54.f4. This is an example of the *Resistance* method involving the attempt to create a strongpoint on f4. This is not a losing move, but I could have maintained a large advantage with either 54.♕a5 or 54.♕a8+ *(Counter-Attack)*. Instead, Black is now fully equal. I went downhill after 54.f4 ♕e6 55.fxg5? (I was so concerned about him opening the g-file with ...gxf4 that I impulsively played this move) 55...♕xe3 and White is lost.

Instead of only considering a passive "resistance" move (54.f4), I failed to look for candidate moves that provide counter-attacking opportunities. For example: 54.♕a8+ ♔g7 55.♕d8!, attacking Black's g-pawn. This queen maneuver is similar to those in Positions T1 and T6. Or 54.♕a5 (threatening ♕d8+) 54...♘f6 55.♕a8+ ♔g7 56.h4!, and White has blunted Black's kingside initiative and is now the one who is attacking!

So the lesson here is that you must take those deep breaths and then look for at least three candidate moves, especially for any which provide counterplay rather than a purely passive defense. Notice that neither of the variations above is very long. In both cases you only need to see 2-3 moves ahead. So in these situations, the ability to calculate is less important than the search for candidate moves and then "visualizing" (rather than analyzing) the targets in the opponent's position after you make that first counter-attacking move (e.g., the g5-pawn is a target in Black's position in both of the variations above).

T8: Black to Move

At the 2000 New York Open, I had Black in Round 5 against Stanislav Kriventsov. At the time of this game he was rated 2440 (USCF) and one year later became an international master. We reached this position after his 15th move:

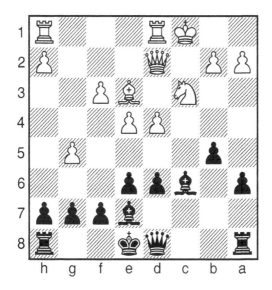

Evaluate the position (is Black worse, equal, or better?) and identify the best move for Black.

Discussion

At this point I felt that White was better because of his strong pawn center and uncertainty about my king's safety, since castling in either direction seemed dangerous. So I decided to hold off on castling and played 15...b4 (the best move) followed by 16...d5 (the best move). Those two moves perfectly balanced *Counter-Attack* (...b5-b4) with passive stabilization (the strong point on d5), enabling me to wait on the decision of where to put my king. White mistakenly closed the position with 17.e5 and drifted slowly into *Zugzwang* over the next 14 moves:

15...b4 16.♘e2 d5 17.e5 ♗a4 18.b3 ♗b5 19.h4 a5 20.♔b1 a4 21.♘c1 axb3 22.♘xb3 ♗c4 23.♕c2 ♕b6 24.♗c1 ♔d7 25.♖he1 ♖hc8 26.♖e3 ♕a6 27.♖d2 ♗f1 28.♕b2 ♗h3 29.♖e1 ♗f5+ 30.♔a1 ♖c3 31.♖ee2 ♕c4 **0-1**

Some lessons from this game:

- Avoid castling too quickly when the position offers opportunities to make other "necessary" moves first (i.e., those that are essential to play as soon as possible). My counter-attack had reached winning proportions by the time I finally moved my king on move 24!

- Active defensive methods are essential in many openings. The Open Sicilian seen in this game is a perfect example. Passive methods of defense in these openings are almost always fatal. So focus mostly on the methods of *Activity, Counter-Attack,* and *Transformation* in these openings (and in positions with asymmetrical piece placement and pawn structures). For example, the move 17...♗a4! is an active counter-attacking move with the idea of coaxing White to play b2-b3. This was the key to the successful counter-attack because the pawn on b3 gives Black a "hook" for his a-pawn to pry open the a-file;

- When defending, especially against a higher-rated player, don't allow overall negative evaluations of the position based on vague feelings to influence your choice of candidate moves. After White played 15.d4, it was not objectively clear to me why my position was worse (in fact, it was better!). Since it was nothing more than a vague feeling, I told myself to put that aside and "just get on with it." That positive mindset gave me the confidence to play aggressively on the queenside and build an unstoppable attack very quickly.

T9: Black to Move

In a 2016 FIDE tournament in New York, I was Black against FIDE Master David Brodsky. He became an IM a year later. We reached this position after White moved his bishop from e3 to f4:

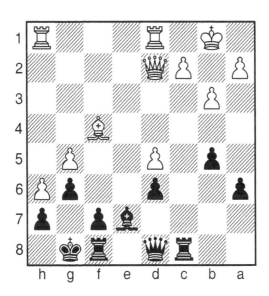

What is Black's best move?

A. ...♕c7
B. ...f6
C. ...♖e8
D. ...♕d7

Discussion

Black needs to relieve the potential mating threats on his g7 square and get some air for his pieces. So the *Activity* method of defense comes to mind as the best approach, since there is no way to increase the counter-attacking pressure on White's g5-pawn. Therefore, the best move is ...f7-f6. The other three alternatives are too passive. Playing "waiting" moves in positions like this against a higher-rated player almost always leads to a slow death. Note that after ...f7-f6, three of Black's pieces are mobilized behind that pawn, ready to unleash their energy. That move gives Black an equal position.

T10: Black to Move

White has sacrificed a lot of material to reach this position in Fressinet – Kempinski, Bundesliga 2009. It appears that Black is about to be checkmated, so it's obvious that the second player has two options: Either resign or find the "only move" to prolong the game. Begin by identifying all candidate moves that prevent White from checkmating on the next move with ♖c3-h3. There are three candidates. Did you find all three?

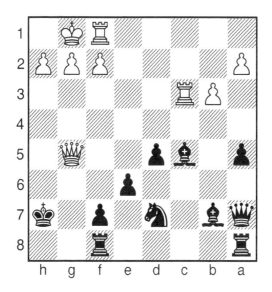

Discussion

The solution is 1...♝e3! 2.♜xe3 (2.fxe3 loses for White) 2...♛xe3 3.fxe3 f6 and the position is equal!

This type of *Only Move* thinking is valuable even when we're not faced with immediate mate. Anytime you're in a difficult defensive position or under a lot of pressure, you must get in the habit of identifying (but not yet evaluating) every reasonable candidate move instead of diving into the one that first captures your attention. This should take no more than 60 seconds in most cases.

When our emotions are heightened, we have a tendency to narrow our search. In these situations, we need a method (the search for multiple candidate moves) that allows us to obtain a more objective view of our defensive possibilities.

As we discussed in the Introduction, our emotions can cloud our judgment, leading to mistakes and blunders. Similar to a drunk driver, in these situations we need to switch over to auto-pilot (the structured methods covered in this book) to safely handle dangerous "road conditions" at the chessboard.

T11: Black to Move

As noted in the previous position, when we're faced with threats that appear to be unstoppable, our first order of business is to identify all of the reasonable candidate moves, instead of immediately going down a "rabbit hole" by starting to analyze the first idea that captures our attention. Below is a good example (Bhend – Lombardy, Zürich 1961). First, what potential moves grab your attention? Second, which one did you choose?

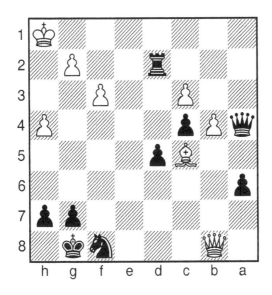

Discussion

There are two possibilities: 1...♔f7 (to run away from the threatened mate) and 1...♕d1+. I quickly dismissed 1...♕d1+ since I didn't see a good follow-up after White plays 2.♔h2. It appeared to be nothing more than a spite check since White is still threatening mate on the move. So I concluded I have "no choice" but to run away with 1...♔f7.

However, the simple follow-up to 1...♕d1+ was the winning move 2...♕xf3. Now I'm threatening mate in one while simultaneously defending the knight on f8! So I was suffering from a case of chess blindness when I rejected 1...♕d1+. When we're facing strong threats, these blind spots are more likely to occur, especially if we're feeling strong emotions. In these cases, we need to take extra time to perform what I call a "15-second Freeze Frame."

After 1...♕d1+, Black should have taken one more step and noticed ...♕d1xf3 since it guards the knight on f8, even though the first impression is that this move just loses the queen. By freeze-framing the position in my mind after ...♕xf3 and closely observing it for at least 15 seconds, I would have noticed that the queen can't be captured! When we're not thinking clearly, we miss such "obvious" moves. In these cases, we need to stop the action by more carefully "seeing" (freeze-framing) the position on the board.

T12: Black to Move

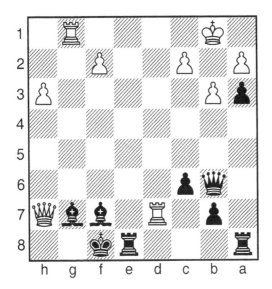

Find three candidate moves for Black and choose the best one.

Discussion

A quick look at White's vicious attack indicates that this is an *Only Move* situation for Black. The only move to save Black is 1...♖e1+!. After White captures the rook (2.♖xe1), Black plays 2...♕xf2 with a large advantage. Be honest: How many candidate moves did you identify prior to making your move? The fact that Black has such a huge material advantage should have been the clue to finding the sacrificial move 1...♖e1+. When you're up a lot of material and under severe pressure, the first question you should ask yourself is, "can I sacrifice some material to shake off the attack and then take advantage of my remaining material edge?"

T13: Black to Move

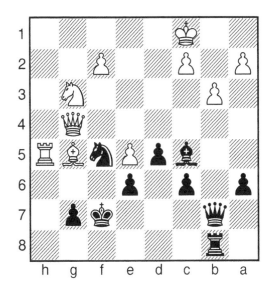

Find three candidate moves for Black and choose the best one.

Discussion

In this game I had Black against NM Dragan Milovanovic (USCF 2270 at the time of this game). He has a strong attack on my kingside and is threatening ♘xf5, the only piece defending my king! So I decided to counter-attack by playing 1...♗a3+. This misplaces my bishop and wastes a precious tempo, giving White a large advantage. The correct move is 1...♛b4!, forcing the exchange of queens. If White avoids the exchange by playing 2.♛e2, Black gets a large advantage with 2...♛d4.

So *Restraint* was the right method here. 1...♛b4 severely restrains White's options and puts a strong brake on his attack. I played 1...♗a3+ impulsively. My emotions were heightened and I didn't take the time to consider any alternatives. Had I sat there patiently (while breathing deeply and slowly) for 60 seconds and looked for 2-3 candidate moves, 1...♛b4 would most certainly have been among them.

Even if it was on my list of candidate moves, I may not have played it, but by not even considering it, the odds of my choosing it were exactly zero! Identifying candidate moves will not always save us when we're defending, but they will dramatically increase our odds of success.

T14: Black to Move

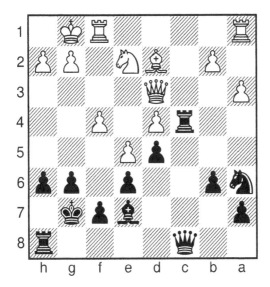

Find three candidate moves for Black and choose the best one.

Discussion

I was Black in this position against NM Victor Levine at the 2000 Liberty Bell Open in Philadelphia. I played 1...f5 in an attempt to either block the kingside, or gain counterplay against his isolated d-pawn after 2.exf6 e.p. ♗xf6. Black's position is not strong enough to play this aggressively. After I recaptured the pawn with 2...♗xf6, White played 3.g4 and obtained a large advantage based on his kingside attack. Had I taken the time to consider less-aggressive defensive methods, I would have noticed that 1...h5! is a strong *Prevention* move that stops White from playing g2-g4. That move gives Black an equal position.

T15: Black to Move

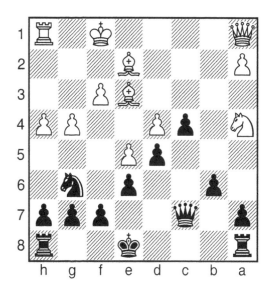

As mentioned in the Introduction, one of the most essential defensive skills is scanning for potential candidate moves before diving into the first one that captures your attention. The primary reason we often fail to consider enough candidate moves when under pressure is that our heightened emotional state creates a "fight-or-flight" mindset. In these cases, we get so focused on the opponent's direct threats that we narrow our attention span significantly.

Think of the quarterback in football who sees the charging defensive lineman coming at him from the front but gets sacked by another player speeding towards him from the side. Recall how I was blindsided in this manner when I overlooked White's threat of ♕a7+ in Position T4.

Find three candidate moves for Black and choose the best one.

Discussion

In this position, reasonable candidate moves include 1...h6 *(Restraining* White's pawn advance); 1...♘e7 *(Prevention* of an attack on Black's knight); and 1...h5 (a combination of *Restraint* and *Counter-Attack).* How many of these candidate moves did you consider?

The best move is 1...h5. It gives Black a small edge. It stops White's h-pawn dead in its tracks and secures the position of the g6-knight. For those readers who found at least three candidate moves with 1...h5 among them, most likely many of you chose it as the best move. For those of you who only considered one move and then decided it was best, most likely far fewer of you chose 1...h5.

It's like the difference between a multiple-choice test and one that requires you to write the correct answer. Most people will agree that multiple-choice tests are easier than "correct answer" tests because choosing among alternatives is easier than providing the correct answer when you're not sure of the answer. So think of candidate moves as giving you an opportunity to change the "test" (chess position) into a multiple-choice format! That increases the odds of finding the best move. Keep in mind that even in tense defensive positions, it does not take long (usually less than 60 seconds) to identify two or three reasonable candidate moves.

T16: Black to Move

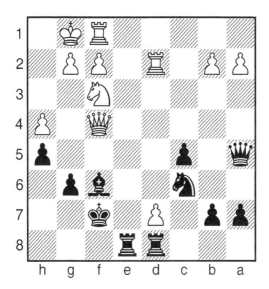

Find three candidate moves for Black and choose the best one.

Discussion

Black is a piece up but under enormous pressure. It doesn't take long to realize that only one or two of the P-R-O-A-C-T defensive methods can potentially save Black: *Only Move* and *Transformation*. An example of a transformation move here is 1...♖e5, sacrificing the exchange to help defuse the attack.

As it turns out, this is an "only move" situation. One move gives Black an equal position and all others lead to a losing position. That move is 1...♖f8!. Feel free to use your chess engine to see why the alternatives are suicidal.

Did you select 1...♖f8 as best? Again, taking the time to find reasonable candidate moves is essential in "only move" situations. Be honest: How many candidate moves did you consider before deciding what to play? If less than three, then you failed to convert this "test" into multiple-choice format. If you chose 1...♖f8 but did not consider any alternatives – nice work, but that "one answer" approach will lead to more wrong answers over time than will a multiple-choice approach based on finding candidate moves.

Rarely will you need to find more than three candidate moves. Keep in mind that while you're looking for candidate moves you should not start analyzing any of them until you have your list. So the process of finding (but not yet analyzing) candidate moves is fairly quick. It's the single most important habit in your toolkit for defending when under pressure.

T17: Black to Move

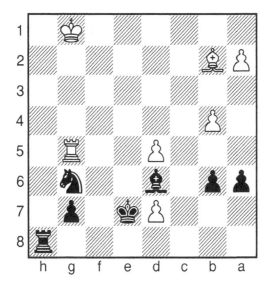

Find three candidate moves for Black and choose the best one.

Discussion

I reached this position with Black against IM Jay Bonin in a 2016 event at the Marshall Chess Club in Manhattan. At this point I had been defending for a long time and my energy level was low. Since I didn't want to ruin what I thought was a drawn position, I decided to "play it safe" by moving 37...♗f7. As I expected, he replied 38.♖f5+ and we repeated the position (a drawn game by threefold repetition).

So my "play it safe" mindset was a form of self-talk that let my opponent off the hook. It led me to consider only cautious moves. I briefly saw 37...♗h2+ but then immediately rejected it by telling myself that this was nothing more than a spite check that does not deal with his threats. It vanished from consideration because I passed judgment on it too quickly. However, since it was a checking move, it was in essence a "free" move (e.g., Topalov could have played the "free" move ...♕d5+ against Carlsen in Position T6).

I call these free moves "pre-candidates" because the real candidates occur after your opponent responds to your free move (e.g., after Carlsen got out of check, one of Topalov's candidate moves was ...e6-e5). So 37...♗h2+ should have stayed on my list of candidates. That would have enabled me to visualize the potential follow-ups to that move. In fact, it is the only one that gives me a winning position. A likely line is 37...♗h2+ 38.♔f2 (or 38.♔g2 ♘f4+ 39.♔f3 ♘h5) 38...♖f8+ 39.♔e1 ♘f4 40.♗xg7 ♖f7 followed by the capture of White's d-pawn.

So in addition to not considering a sufficient number of candidate moves when under pressure, we often see the best move for a split second but then reject it impulsively because it doesn't fit our perception of the position. However, any moves that deliver check should make the list of candidate moves simply because of their forcing nature. So the key is not to let those pre-candidate moves vanish from our mind.

There is no doubt that Topalov saw ...♕d5+ since it was clearly an "only move" situation and a checking move is the most obvious one to consider in such cases. He just didn't take the time to visualize the squares controlled by the queen from d5. Instead, ...♕d5+ vanished from his mind. His pawn on e6 "blocked his view" of the critical g8 square. Had that pawn been on e5 instead of e6 when he resigned, I believe he would have seen immediately that ...♕d5+ allows him to defend successfully and achieve an equal position. So this was not an analytical error on his part, but a failure of visualization.

T18: Black to Move

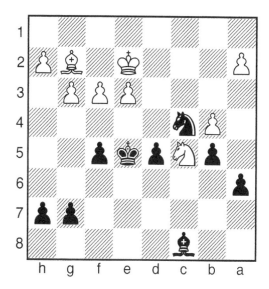

Find three candidate moves for Black and choose the best one.

Discussion

I was Black here against IM Dean Ippolito in a rated event in New Jersey in 2010. In positions like this with good drawing chances, the natural tendency against a strong opponent is to "play it safe" and just try not to make any blunders. However, avoiding blunders in roughly equal positions is not sufficient against strong players. Numerous 2700-rated GMs have been outplayed by Magnus Carlsen in equal endgames without making any obvious mistakes. It's possible to slowly drift into a lost position without realizing it until it's too late. So vigilance is required.

Believe it or not, only one move here gives Black a completely equal (0.00) position. The three "next best" moves give White a small plus. So the first instinct should be to look for *Activity* (the "A" in P-R-O-A-C-T). The most obvious active candidate move is 48...a5, seeking to eliminate the queenside pawns. I played that move and, after 49.bxa5 ♘xa5, the game was drawn a few moves later.

The lesson here is that passivity can be deadly. Only use a cautious method of defense (P-R-O) when it's clear you have no choice. Always consider the most active methods (A-C-T) first to avoid drifting into a lost position.

T19: Black to Move

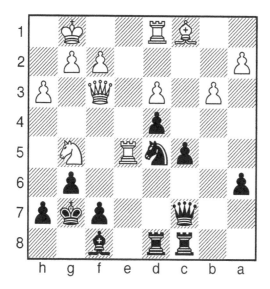

Find three candidate moves for Black and choose the best one.

Discussion

I was Black in this position against a lower-rated player in a rated event in Atlanta. White has the obvious threat of ♖xd5. Instead of considering at least three candidate moves, I quickly played 1...♘f6 based on the reasoning that my knight is attacked and my king needs more defenders, so therefore the best move is the "obvious" ...♘f6. White then played 2.♖e6!. That move not only created an immediate threat of capturing the knight I had just moved to f6, but it clears the e5 square for White to attack my queen with ♗f4! followed by ♗e5+. After I played 2...♘g8 to save my knight, those moves led to a quick checkmate for White.

Instead of 1...♘f6, either 1...♕d7 or 1...♕b7 would have given me a roughly equal position. Both are obvious candidate moves to deal with the threat of ♖xd5 while keeping my knight in an active position. In addition, they remove potential fork tricks on e6 involving my king and queen and also prevent (the "P" in P-R-O-A-C-T) the ♗c1-f4 attack on my queen that occurred in the game.

So either of those queen moves would have eliminated *three* threats! 1...♘f6 and 2...♘g8 were not "blunders" since they did not hang any material, but they were highly passive moves containing serious tactical oversights that allowed White to achieve a winning position. So they were the equivalent of blunders in terms of their negative impact on my position.

The lesson here is that good defensive moves (e.g., 1...♕d7 or 1...♕b7) are usually not hard to find and often do not require a lot of calculation, as long as we take the time to look for several candidate moves. When we play the first move that catches our eye and it seems to have some merit (e.g., "1...♘f6 defends my knight on d5 and helps protect my king"), the likelihood of defending successfully drops significantly.

T20: Black to Move

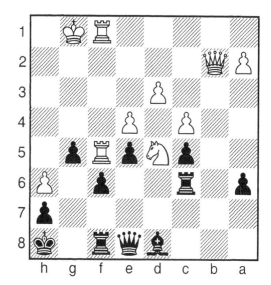

This is a variation from my game at the Marshall Chess Club against Asa Hoffman, a life master and a legend in the New York area who played many blitz games with Bobby Fischer when they were teenagers.

Among the P-R-O-A-C-T defensive methods, a blend of *Restraint* and *Activity* appears to be the best approach here. Find three candidate moves for Black in this position and then choose the best one.

Discussion

Hoffman (White) looks much better here, but he has only a small advantage according to both *Fritz* 16 and *Stockfish* 10.

One candidate move is 42...♛e6. Did you consider it? If so, did you evaluate it to be a good move or a poor one? Notice after that move that White is threatening both 43.♖g5 and 43.♛e5 winning a pawn since my f6-pawn is pinned. The move 42...♛e6 does not prevent either threat. However, if White plays either reply, Black's position is freed up. For example: 43.♛xe5 fxe5 44.♖xf8+ ♛g8 45.♖xg8+ ♔xg8. Notice that material is even and White's pawn on h6 will soon fall. Or 43.♖g5 ♛h3! when Black has massive counterplay and White can't capture the e5-pawn with the rook or the queen (44.♖xe5 loses to 44...♖g8+ and 44.♛xe5 loses to 44... ♛f1+). Also, notice that the g-file is now open, so White's king is much less secure than before.

This solution involved the *Activity* (...♛e6) method of defense. Black was willing to "let" White win either the e5- or the g5-pawn in exchange for freeing himself from a cramped, passive position. White should avoid the bait and not take either pawn after ...♛e6. Passive attempts by Black to hold the position were doomed to fail, as White will eventually break through if Black doesn't take action to free his game. In this example it was the only move to give Black near-equality.

So the sequence for handling passive positions is to remind yourself to consider all potential P-R-O-A-C-T methods, especially the *Activity* and *Counter-Attack* methods. That will alert you to look for moves like 42... ♛e6 that you otherwise would have missed completely, or would have rejected because "that move allows my opponent to win a pawn." When we're in a passive bind like I was here, greedily trying to hang on to your extra pawn against a stronger player almost always leads to a lost game.

T21: Black to Move

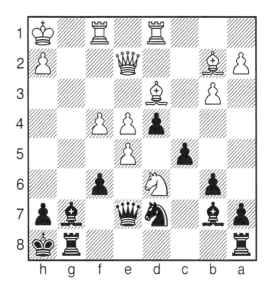

Find three candidate moves for Black and then pick the best one.

Discussion

Black is under a lot of pressure. The first instinct is to protect the b7-bishop since that is the most obvious threat. However, did you notice that White is also threatening a massive kingside attack involving ♗d3-c4, ♘d6-f5, and a transfer of his queen and rook to the g-file? If you did, then you probably realized the need to consider active (A-C-T: *Activity, Counter-Attack,* or *Transformative)* moves.

In fact, the *Transformative* move 1...fxe5 is the only one to give Black an equal game. Best play runs 1...fxe5 2.♘xb7 exf4 3.♖xf4 ♘e5 (notice that White's knight has no escape squares) 4.♗a6 ♖gb8, followed by ...♖b8-b7.

The two primary clues that active defensive (A-C-T) moves are required instead of purely passive (P-R-O) ones are the presence of pawn tension and when your opponent's pieces are much more active than yours. Notice in this position how all of Black's pieces are on his first two ranks. When both of these clues are present, there's a high probability that your opponent has more than one threat – an immediate one (such as the unprotected black bishop on b7 in this example) and "imminent" (near-term) threats such as a strong kingside attack. Passive methods rarely work when we're faced with both immediate and imminent threats.

By playing 1...fxe5, Black transforms the position. For a small sacrifice of material in the line above, the second player achieves a roughly equal game. White's pressure and kingside attacking chances have vanished.

Sometimes *Transformative* moves are desperate attempts to confuse the opponent when our position is lost. However, this is an example where *Transformative* thinking is a bridge to a dynamically equal position. Transformative defense leading to dynamic equality is the most difficult form of defense because it involves far more calculation than the other five methods.

T22: Black to Move

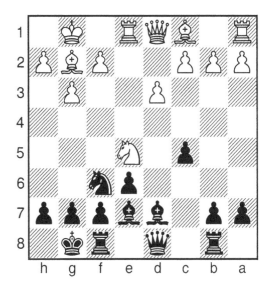

I was Black in this position against NM (national master) Yevgeny Feldman (USCF 2320 at the time of this game) in an event at the Marshall Chess Club. Identify three candidate moves for Black and then choose the best one.

Discussion

There is no clearly best move here. The main candidates are ...♗e8, ...♕c7, ...♗d6, and ...b7-b5. All are roughly equal. If you chose any of the last three alternatives but did not consider ...♗e8 at all, then you get 90% credit for solving the position instead of 100%. My reasoning for this scoring "penalty" is that by not considering ...♗e8, you did not give sufficient attention to *Prevention* since White could now win the bishop pair with ♘xd7.

This is a fairly open position where the bishop pair in the hands of a strong player gives White long-term opportunities to outplay his opponent, especially in an endgame with pawns on both sides of the board. I played ...♗e8 for that reason. It's only a temporary inconvenience for Black since now he can challenge the white knight on e5 by playing ...♘f6-d7 at some point.

T23: Black to Move

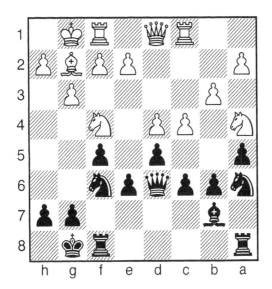

I had Black in this position against GM Ildar Ibragimov at the 2003 U.S. Amateur Team Championship. Identify three candidate moves and then select the best one.

Discussion

The main candidates are ...b6-b5, ...c6-c5, and ...g7-g5. White has a slight advantage because of Black's pawn weaknesses on e6 and b6. So Black needs to stabilize the position by focusing on cautious (P-R-O) methods of defense. The best move is ...b6-b5, attacking the knight while maintaining my strongpoint on d5. Instead, however, I chose 18...c5 to defend my b6-pawn with my queen while gaining activity in the center. Once I saw those two benefits of playing ...c6-c5, I played it without further thought. However, after 18...c5, play continued 19.dxc5 bxc5 20.cxd5 exd5 21.♕c2 and now White has a double attack on my f5- and c5-pawns.

When we're defending, pawn tension in the position (e.g., the four pawns on d4, c4, d5, and c5) should be an immediate warning sign that there is the potential for multiple pawn exchanges that significantly alter the position. I turned a stable position (i.e., my strongpoint on d5) into a dynamic one with one simple pawn move. The lesson here is that any time you are considering a move that increases the pawn tension when you're defending, you must first ask yourself: "Am I triggering a potential chain reaction of exchanges that are unfavorable for me?" The only way to answer that question is through concrete calculation of variations 3-4 moves deep. In the example above, calculating those three additional moves before I played ...c6-c5 would not have been difficult.

T24: Black to Move

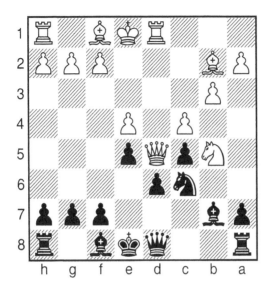

This is another position where I was Black against NM Yevgeny Feldman (USCF 2300), this time in a 2013 FIDE event at the Marshall Chess Club. Find at least two candidate moves and then choose the best one.

Discussion

When our opponent appears to have an unstoppable threat, that's a warning sign that we need to fully activate our "tactical antennae." What I mean by that is that the threat can't be met by a single direct defensive move, so we need to rely on indirect defense by looking for active alternatives that consist of a short series of moves involving exchanges that successfully meet the threat.

So the question to ask yourself in these situations is: How can I "allow" my opponent to carry out his threat in a way that I can exploit two or three moves later? Once you frame the situation that way, it's not too hard to notice the candidate move ...♕b6 (the best move). Fortunately, I played this move. Visualize for yourself that the d6-pawn is now poisoned, so it can't be captured. Black is fully equal.

T25: Black to Move

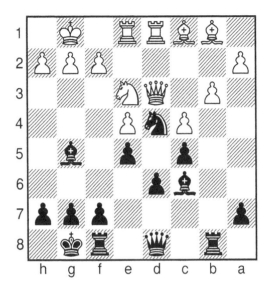

Find three candidate moves for Black and select the best one.

Discussion

This position is a few moves later in my game (T24) against Yevgeny Feldman. Black has a solid defensive position and is fully developed. Nevertheless, that does not mean he should become overly cautious in an attempt to achieve a draw against a higher-rated player. When we know we have a solid, equal position against a higher-rated player, we *must* play active moves when the position warrants it. If we don't seize those moments, in the vast majority of cases we will be slowly outplayed.

Since Black is not under pressure in this position, his first instinct should be to look for active moves. Once you have that awareness, the move ...a7-a5 is easy to find. It starts a minority attack on the queenside and gives Black a slight edge. I played that move and made several more "active" decisions during the rest of the game, resulting in a hard-fought draw. The lesson here is that overly passive or cautious moves in equal positions against stronger players is extremely dangerous, especially in positions with asymmetrical pawn structures. More often than not, we'll slowly get outplayed.

T26: Black to Move

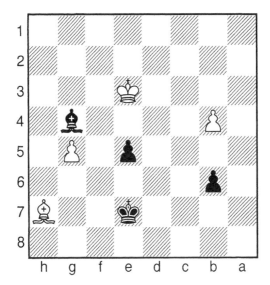

Find three candidate moves for Black and choose the best one.

Discussion

I was Black in this position against Abhimanyu Mishra in a rated event in New Jersey in 2017. Less than two years after this game, he became the youngest international master in chess history at the age of 10 years and nine months. Then in June 2021, he became the youngest grandmaster ever at the age of 12 years and four months. His stated goal is to become world champion!

White has a small advantage here and Black needs to be careful to hold the position. The moves ...♗d1, ...♗e6, and ...♔d6 are the best candidates. Thinking that I could make any reasonable "waiting" move, I quickly played 1...♗h3. This gives White a completely winning position after 2.♔e4. When we're in a heightened emotional state and/or we're short on time, "rules of thumb" to guide us in selecting a move become essential.

One rule of thumb in these situations is to consider moves that maximize mobility and centralization when we don't have time to calculate variations. In this position, 1...♗h3 totally violates that rule. It puts my bishop on the edge of the board where its mobility is severely limited. This rule of thumb helps us find moves like 1...♗d1, which prevents White from moving his king to e4 (due to the ...♗c2+ skewer). Or if White plays 2.g6, then Black plays 2...♗c2! to pin the g-pawn against the bishop on h7.

T27: White to Move

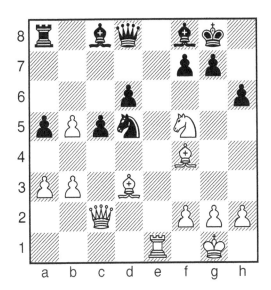

I was White against NM Dragan Milovanovic in a 2017 event in New Jersey. Find three candidate moves and choose the best one.

Discussion

I'm a positional player, so my instinct is to play cautious moves when defending or when opponents play moves containing a threat. So my ability to find P-R-O defensive moves is much higher than my ability to find A-C-T moves. Readers who are tactical players have the opposite problem. Therefore, in this position I quickly chose the "safe" 1.♗g3. It's the second-best move and gives me a small advantage. Had I forced myself out of my comfort zone by considering at least one aggressive candidate move, I would have taken a close look at 1.♘xd6!. That move gives White a completely winning position.

The variations are not hard to calculate. I dismissed that move immediately because I was so focused on saving my hanging bishop! After 1.♘xd6, Black can't play 1...♘xf4 due to 2.♗h7+ followed by 3.♘xf7#. Or if Black plays 1...♗xd6, then White recaptures with 2.♗xd6 and Black can't take my bishop due to 3.♖e8+ followed by mate in two.

The lesson here is that positional players who prefer to shy away from tactics must get more comfortable with calculating short-range tactics. The way to foster this mindset is to ensure that you consider at least one *Counter-Attack* move when your opponent has an immediate threat.

T28: White to Move

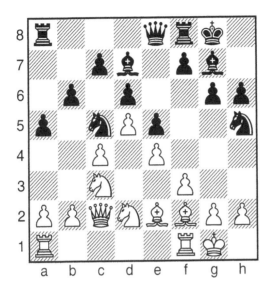

I played White in this game against NM Matthew O'Brien in a 2018 New Jersey event. Find three candidate moves for White and decide on the best one.

Discussion

Black is building up the standard kingside attack in the King's Indian Defense. Before getting on with his queenside attack, White needs to take some precautions. If the black knight is allowed to reach f4, it will be hard to dislodge. A prophylactic genius like Anatoly Karpov would immediately play g2-g3: it not only prevents ...♘f4, but if Black ever plays ...f7-f5-f4, White then can close the kingside with g3-g4 and continue his queenside attack. Since I'm a positional player, I played g2-g3 in the game and we eventually drew.

T29: Black to Move

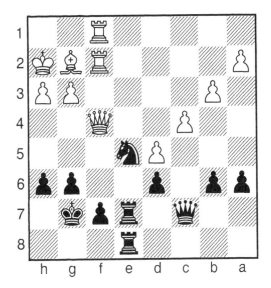

I was Black here against NM Yefim Treger (USCF 2310 at the time of this game) in a Marshall Chess Club competition. Find three candidate moves for Black and choose the best one.

Discussion

Treger was rated 200 points higher than me when this game took place and was known as a brilliant attacker and tactician (the exact opposite style from mine). However, I felt the position was equal because of my unassailable knight on e5 and my kingside pawn majority. So I sensed that the position called for an active move, especially since passive moves against a player like Treger are usually doomed to failure. Those thoughts led me to "get on with it" and play 28...f5, keeping his pieces out of f6 and gaining space on the kingside with my pawn majority. That was the correct move and it gives Black a small plus.

If you didn't consider that move because you were afraid of 29.g4 fxg4 30.♕f6+ ♔h7, or just thought the move was too risky, you were the victim of amygdala hijacking (i.e., your fear short-circuited the logical part of your brain and quickly steered you in a "safer" direction).

The lesson here is that any time our emotions are heightened and we're aware that we can't think clearly and logically, it's time to take several deep breaths and consider a mix of cautious and active candidate moves. Most players know that pawn majorities need to be mobilized, especially against a stronger opponent who will eventually outplay us if we simply try to hold an equal position with "safe" moves.

T30: Black to Move

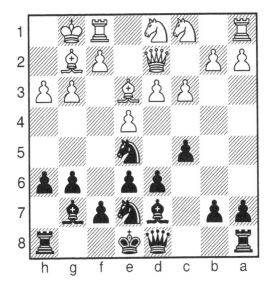

I have Black here against NM Shear McClelland (USCF 2267) at a 2001 event in New York City. Find three candidate moves and choose the best one.

Discussion

When we anticipate that our opponent is about to start a pawn storm (e.g., f2-f4 and/or d3-d4 here), often the best defensive method is to seek counterplay and gain space by moving a pawn into position to exchange one of the storming pawns. In this position, that move is 22...g5!. Then, after 23.f4 gxf4 24.gxf4 ♞5g6, Black has opened the g-file for potential counterplay and also swapped off one of the storming pawns. Following these moves, I had a fully equal position.

You've come across this lesson several times already: We need to seek activity in fluid positions where both sides have mobile pawns. In these situations, excess caution will usually fail against a higher-rated player.

T31: White to Move

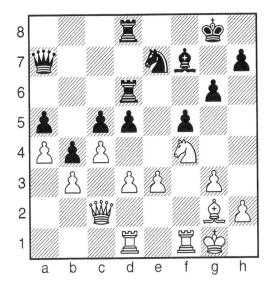

Find three candidate moves for White and pick the best one.

Discussion

In the 2001 New Jersey State Championship, I was White in this position against IM Dean Ippolito. Though the game is equal, Dean's position is much easier to play because of the buildup of major pieces behind his d-pawn. A pawn exchange at the right moment would unleash a lot of pressure on White's position. However, as I've mentioned several times already, passive or overly cautious moves against a much stronger player usually lead to certain death. So in these cases you must at least consider active candidate moves along with more solid, cautious ones.

With this in mind I played 26.e4, seeking to resolve the tension in the center through the exchange of a couple of pawns, expecting that this would be followed by the trade of one or more major pieces. The only concern I had before making my move was that after 26.e4 fxe4 27.dxe4, Black could play 27...d4 and obtain a protected passed pawn while leaving me with an isolated e-pawn.

But then I noticed I could immediately play 28.e5!. That looked good to me and *Stockfish* agrees that it gives White a large advantage. In the actual game, these were the next several moves: 26.e4 dxe4 27.dxe4 fxe4 28.♖xd6 ♖xd6 29.♗xe4 ♕d7 30.♕f2 ♘f5 31.♘d5 ♕e6 32.♗xf5 gxf5 33.♕xc5, and White is winning. I played mistake-free for the rest of the game and Black resigned after 65 moves.

26.e4 is not the only good move in this position. There are at least three others that *Stockfish* evaluates as similar in strength. However, if you only looked at "safe" candidate moves in an attempt to just hold the position and didn't consider e3-e4 at all or rejected it quickly because it looked too risky, you did not "solve" the position as well as someone who at least seriously considered this move.

I'll repeat myself: Unless there is no alternative, passive "hold the fort" moves against much stronger players almost never succeed. By playing the active e3-e4, I increased the tension and changed the nature of the position without taking any unnecessary risks. My 2450-rated opponent had an off-day and didn't handle the heightened activity well. Had I "played it safe" with a move like 26.♕c1 or 26.♗f3, most likely I would have been gradually outplayed.

T32: Black to Move

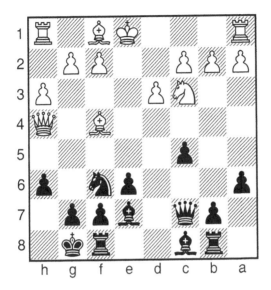

Find three candidate moves for Black and choose the best one.

Discussion

I was Black against NM Yefim Treger (then rated USCF 2320) in a Swiss System tournament at the Marshall Chess Club. My last move was ...h7-h6 and his reply was ♗f4, reaching the position in the diagram. I quickly rejected ...e6-e5 because I wanted to keep the solid pawn structure on the kingside and play ...b7-b5 followed by ...♗c8-b7 with a fantastic diagonal for my bishop. As a positional player, I was captivated by the long-range power of that bishop! In contrast, ...e6-e5 did not appear to have any merits other than chasing away White's bishop.

So I quickly played 1...♗d6 and Treger immediately played 2.♗xh6!. I was stunned and hadn't noticed that moving my bishop from e7 to d6 leaves my knight unprotected. In this emotional state, I immediately captured his bishop (2...gxh6) and he replied 3.♕xf6. He was now a pawn up and my kingside structure was in shambles. But the real mistake was not 1...♗d6, but the "obvious" capture 2...gxh6. A much better reply is 2...♗e5. This keeps my kingside pawn structure intact and puts pressure on White's position. Both *Stockfish* 11 and *Fritz* 16 evaluate the position after 2...♗e5 as dead equal! Black is fully developed and White's king is unsafe.

The lesson here is that when you are shocked by your opponent's move, especially one involving a capture, you should *never* recapture immediately. You must first take several deep breaths and sit on your hands for at least 30 seconds until the shock wears off. Only then should you consider what to play. Had I done that, I would have seen that 2...♗e5 was a much better move because it activates my bishop and keeps a solid pawn structure in front of my king.

When we're in a heightened emotional state, our "Chess IQ" temporarily drops by a large amount. It's like trying to pass a driving test on an obstacle course while intoxicated! So we must first "get sober" (i.e., take deep breaths and sit on our hands) before responding to these shocking moves.

T33: Black to Move

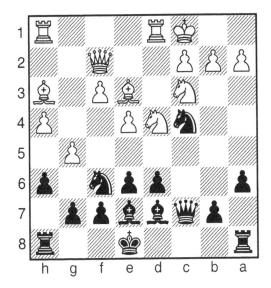

I had Black in this game against NM Mauricio Uribe in a Marshall Chess Club event. Quickly look for at least three candidate moves using the P-R-O-A-C-T list of methods to insure you have a mix of cautious and active choices. Then figure out which one is best.

Discussion

In the game it took me about 30 seconds to find what I thought were the three best candidate moves: 1...hxg5, 1...♘h5, and 1...♘xe3. I quickly rejected the first two because they seemed too passive and I was concerned that after 1...♘h5, White could reply 2.g6, hitting the f-pawn that is guarding my e6-pawn. By capturing White's bishop on e3, I felt I was eliminating his very active bishop while also gaining the bishop pair. Talk about superficial thinking! That knight was perfectly positioned to support a counter-attack starting with ...♕b6 threatening immediate mate. If White defends with b2-b3, Black can reply ...♕b6-a5 and continue his queenside attack.

Also, I could have played 1...♘h5 in the diagram position while retaining the threat of ...♕c7-b6! So both 1...♘h5 and 1...♕b6 give Black a completely equal position. Instead, 1...♘xe3 swapped off my only active piece. It had moved four times to capture a piece that had moved only once. Only rarely can Black get away with losing that many tempi in the Open Sicilian.

I'll bet that most players who notice the possibility of playing 1...♕b6 in this position will choose it over other candidate moves. Once you see it, it becomes an obvious choice. Being disciplined in looking for multiple candidate moves is the key to finding non-obvious resources when defending under pressure. Remember that a multiple-choice test is easier than one that requires you to answer without any hints. So you should always seek to turn defensive situations into a multiple-choice test by mentally noting all reasonable candidate moves before evaluating the first one that captures your attention.

T34: Black to Move

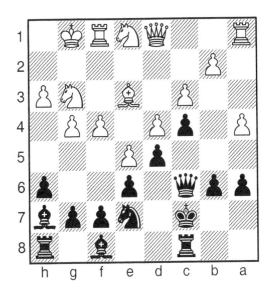

Here I played Black against NM Mark Kernighan (USCF 2270 at the time of this game) in a New Jersey tournament from 2016. Find three candidate moves and then select the best choice. White's buildup on the kingside should be a warning bell that you need to consider ways to restrain (the "R" in P-R-O-A-C-T) his pawn storm.

Discussion

Your list should have included such candidates as 1...♔b7, 1...♕d7, 1...f6, and 1...f5. All are solid moves. However, both *Stockfish* and *Fritz* view 1...f5 as slightly better than the other three. That is the move I chose. White captured *en passant* (2.exf6) and I recaptured (2...gxf6). So you might be asking yourself why 1...f6 isn't considered as good as 1...f5 since they both lead to the same outcome. Take a moment to try to answer that question before I explain.

The main difference is that if Black played 1...f6, it would give White the option of playing the aggressive 2.f5. By playing 1...f5 instead, Black either achieves a blockade on the f5 square, or eliminates the spearhead of White's attack (the e5-pawn) should White capture *en passant*. That would also open the g-file for Black's h8-rook. So the difference between these two moves is noteworthy.

T35: Black to Move

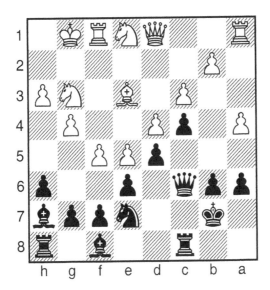

OK, let's imagine that you didn't prevent White from playing f4-f5 in the prior position and after a couple more moves you reach this position as Black. Find three candidate moves and choose the best one.

Discussion

There is more than one good move here. While the position is roughly equal, it's much easier for White to play. In annotations by grandmasters, they will often make this type of comment ("it's not objectively the best move, but I chose it because I thought it would be easier to play") regarding why they chose a particular variation during the game. So in this example, allowing White to play f4-f5 is not objectively bad since Black still has rough equality, but the move gives the attacker a position that's easier to play compared to his opponent's.

Don't get hung up on the fact that many of the puzzles in this book have more than one acceptable solution. That is not the point of these exercises since this is not a "find the winning move" book. It is a training manual designed to provide thinking tools to help you defend successfully.

The two best moves in this position are the waiting moves 1...♕d7 and 1...♕c7. Since White's pawn storm is well advanced, Black's options are limited to "hold the fort" methods of defense. Rarely is it correct for the defender to capture the pawn that's leading the charge (White's f5-pawn here), especially if the opponent can recapture with a pawn to establish a "pawn duo" on his fifth rank. Instead, the best defensive method for handling advanced pawn storms is patient restraint, waiting for the attacker to overpress or create open lines where we can counter-attack (e.g., Black's knight and his h7-bishop will spring to life via the g6 square if White advances or exchanges his f5-pawn).

Even in positions where White is planning a pawn storm, he sometimes needs to first restrain a potential pawn storm by his opponent before proceeding with his own attack. A perfect example of this is Position T17, where White played the seemingly passive and cautious g2-g3 in anticipation of Black's coming pawn roller and to prevent the black knight from entering the f4 square. Many attacking players are weak in the areas of *Prevention* and *Restraint*. These methods are important for success in both attack and defense, but are much more common in defensive situations.

T36: White to Move

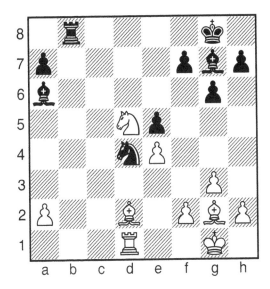

I was White in this position against NM Dan Lapan (USCF 2350) in a 2017 FIDE-rated tournament at the Marshall Chess Club. The position is equal, but easier for Black to play because his rook is already on an open file and his light-squared bishop and knight are exerting coordinated pressure on my kingside. Find three candidate moves and choose the best one.

Discussion

My first instinct was to play 33.♗f1 to contest his bishop's control of the a6-f1 diagonal. That is the best move according to both *Stockfish* and *Fritz*. But I rejected it after superficially "calculating" the line 33.♗f1 ♘f3+ 34.♔g2 ♘xd2 35.♖xd2 ♖b1 "winning my pinned bishop." This was a hallucination. In my sloppy calculation, I forgot that the king was no longer on g1. So in my mind, I "saw" a pin that wasn't real! However, even if my king *were* still on g1, the pin could have been met with ♘d5-e3.

Thus, instead of 33.♗f1, I played the aimless 33.a3. After 33...♗e2 34.♖c1 ♘xf3 35.♗xf3 ♗xf3, Black had won the bishop pair and enjoyed a small but stable advantage. He went on to win the endgame. My original intention (33.♗f1) would have given me a fully equal game.

The lesson here is that anytime we're considering a move that will trigger a series of active moves by the opponent (such as checks and captures), we must use the "15-second Freeze Frame" technique (as discussed in T11) to clearly "see" *each* move of the sequence, not just the final position in the sequence. Typically it's the middle moves in a series that we fail to anchor clearly in our mind. In this example, ♔g1-g2 was the second move in the sequence I calculated, so I didn't take the time to freeze the image of that "middle" move in my mind. Instead, it remained on g1 in my mind as if it had never moved!

The usual advice for handling these tactical sequences is to "double-check" before playing the move that triggers the sequence. That is generally good advice, but if you don't also "freeze-frame" each step in that sequence, double-checking will often not be sufficient to prevent simple oversights and hallucinations.

T37: Black to Move

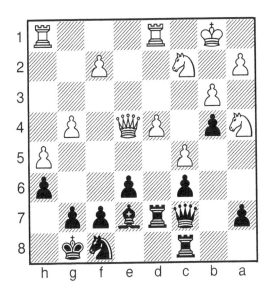

I was Black in this position against Grandmaster Alonso Zapata. It was the last tournament in 2020 at the Atlanta Chess Center before the coronavirus put a stop to all in-person tournaments. After 30 moves the game is equal, but White's position is easier to play. Find three candidate moves and then choose the best one.

Discussion

Reasonable candidate moves include 1...♖b8, 1...♕b7, and 1...♕b8. A less obvious but good candidate is 1...♘h7, "letting" White win the b4-pawn to gain time for a redeployment grouping of the knight to f6 and then d5. Even that move gives Black an equal position. I chose the worst of these four moves (1...♕b7). Now the queen has no mobility and its lowly role is to guard my b4-pawn. White enjoys an edge, though Black is not lost yet. Instead, 1...♖b8 would have given me a completely equal game. My queen remains active on the b8-h2 diagonal and White's only active plan is to play 2.f4, which can be met by 2...♘h7! restraining White's attack.

The lesson here is that passive moves that reduce the mobility of our pieces (especially the queen, as in this example) often lead to a gradual drift into a lost position, especially when facing a much higher-rated player (like a grandmaster!). Since the rook is less powerful than the queen, it and not Her Majesty should have been assigned the duty of guarding my b4-pawn.

So when a cautious move is required as you're defending and you have two or three candidate moves that all appear to work, the rule of thumb is that in most cases the best choice will be the move that maintains more flexibility and mobility than the alternatives. With this rule in mind, it's much easier to see that 1...♖b8 is far better than 1...♕b7.

By this point in the book, I hope the reader will have come to the re-alization that training positions containing multiple reasonable moves increase our skills far more than do puzzles with single-move solutions, especially those with one winning move. Of course we need to find those winning moves in our games, so that type of training remains worthwhile. However, even more important for increasing your rating is to cut down on weak moves and blunders when you *don't* have a winning position. By doing that, you'll have many more games where there is a winning move for you to find!

T38: Black to Move

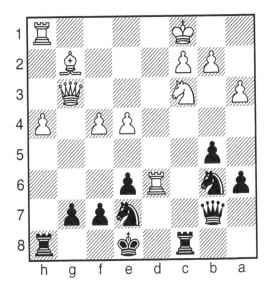

I had Black in this position against NM Juan Sena in a 2013 FIDE-rated competition at the Marshall Chess Club. White appears to have a large advantage due to his extra pawn and my king's being stuck in the center. However, there is one move that gives Black a nearly equal position. Find three candidate moves and identify the best one.

Discussion

In sharp positions like this, there is no time for cautious (P-R-O) moves. Black needs to quickly find counterplay before it's too late! Now that you have this hint, you can probably see that ...b5-b4 is promising since it attacks a piece and opens the b-file toward White's king.

After 18...b4, best play is 19.e5 ♛b8 20.axb4 ♞c4 21.♖a6 ♛b4 22.♖a2 ♞f5 23.♛e1 0-0. Notice how White's rook went from a super-active position on d6 to a passive one on a2! This beautiful counter-attack is similar to the one in Position T22.

T39: Black to Move

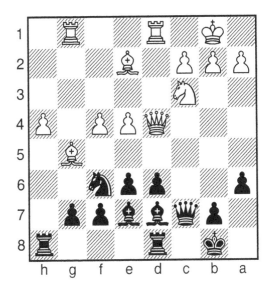

I was Black here against a 1950-rated player in a 2017 event in New Jersey. Identify three candidate moves and then choose the best one.

Discussion

Stockfish and Fritz are in complete agreement that the active ...d6-d5 is the best move and gives Black full equality. If you rejected that move out of fear of the sequence 1...d5 2.e5 ♘g8 3.♗xe7 ♘xe7 4.♖xg7 "winning a pawn and threatening my f7-pawn," your calculation was sloppy since 4.♖xg7 allows 4...♘f5, forking the rook and queen. However, even better after 1...d5 2.e5 is 2...♗c5 forking the queen and rook, although this is not winning for Black because, after 3.♕d3 ♗xg1 4.exf6 gxf6 5.♗xf6 ♗c5, the position is equal. I didn't see the variation involving 2...♗c5, but I did see the one with 2...♘g8 during the game, so I did play 1...d5 and went on to win after an additional 20 moves.

The lesson here is that when we're considering an active move while defending that will trigger a sequence of forcing moves, we must not cut our calculations off too early. This premature rejection of the line will convince us that the active move is not playable. When that happens, we usually wind up playing a passive "waiting" move that is far inferior.

T40: White to Move

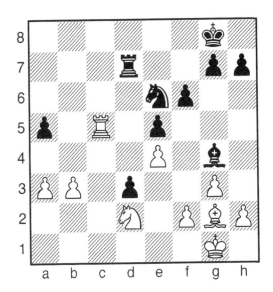

I played White in this position against IM Tim Taylor at a 2014 Marshall Chess Club event. He had the initiative for much of the middlegame, so when we reached this position, I was low on energy after working hard to neutralize his activity. In fact, in this position I have a significant advantage. Find three candidate moves and choose the best one.

Discussion

The obvious candidates are 1.♖a5, 1.♖c8+, 1.♖d5, 1.♖c3, and 1.♖c1. Only one of these moves maintains a large advantage for White. The other four moves pass the advantage over to Black! Given that Black has a far advanced d-pawn, White's priorities are to maintain the blockade on d2 and to prevent Black from activating his rook. So the obvious candidate move is 1.♖c8+. This is a "free" move because of the check.

After Black replies 1...♔f7, White follows up with f2-f3 and then ♗h3 with a huge plus. Instead of 1.♖c8+, I grabbed the a5-pawn and was in deep trouble after Black seized the open c-file that I carelessly abandoned. Both *Fritz* and *Stockfish* agree that Black is now much better. The rest of the game went: 33.♖xa5 ♖c7 34.h3 ♗e2 35.♗f1 ♖c2 36.♘c4 ♖c1 37.♘d2 ♗xf1 38.♘xf1 d2 **0-1**

Awareness of the need for "restraint" (maintaining the blockade of the d3-pawn and keeping the black rook inactive) was required at this moment in the game. So when your energy level is low, that's a warning signal that you need to sit on your hands and not make the first move that catches your eye.

Recall the drunk driver on the obstacle course. He or she needs to "get sober" before there is an accident. Sitting on your hands forces you to muster the attention needed to avoid careless mistakes when your energy is low. When I captured the a5-pawn, it was the equivalent of driving into a ditch. It's an especially tough loss to let an IM escape due to careless driving!

T41: Black to Move

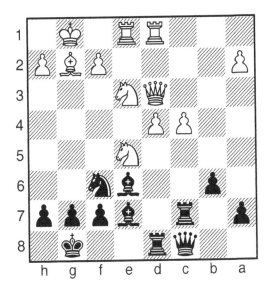

Find three candidate moves for Black. Then choose the best one.

Discussion

I had Black in this position against NM David Grasso at a 2013 FIDE-rated event in New York City. I have a slight advantage thanks to my bishop pair and more compact pawn structure. Both *Stockfish* and *Fritz* agree that Black is slightly better.

If the move 1...b5 was not on your list, evaluate that move now before reading the commentary below.

As a positional player, I couldn't take my eyes off the possibility of playing 1...b5. If White replies 2.c5, I obtain a massive hole on d5 and White's d-pawn is backward on an open file. If he replies 2.cxb5, I again obtain complete control of the d5 square and he has an isolated d-pawn on an open file. So I quickly played 1...b5. However, after 2.cxb5 ♗xa2, he played the obvious 3.♘c6 and I'm busted!

What went wrong here? I evaluated only the positional aspects of the position and did not "freeze-frame" the position in my mind after 2...♗xa2. Prior to 1...b5, the white knight had no access to c6. What I failed to notice is that after he plays 2.cxb5, the c6 square is now protected, allowing the winning knight raid!

The lesson here has appeared in prior positions in this book: When you're considering a move that is almost guaranteed to trigger at least one capture by each player, you need to take a clear look at the placement of the pawns and pieces when the capturing sequence has ended. Try it. Visualize (freeze-frame) the position after 2...♗xa2. Even a beginner can see that with a white pawn on b5, the knight move to c6 is a killer. Since that b-pawn was not part of my positional considerations, its control of the c6 square was invisible to me.

T42: White to Move

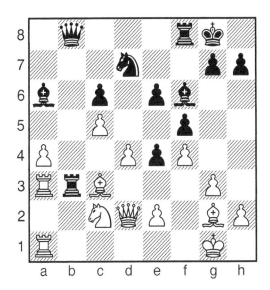

As mentioned in Position T3, I won the U.S. Amateur Championship in 2003. Ten years later I entered the final round of this event with a chance to win the tournament for a second time. In that crucial game, I was White against expert Leonard Chipkin and we reached this position. I have a large advantage. The best moves are 24.♗f1 to activate my bishop and 24.e3 to strengthen my center.

Instead, I quickly played 24.♘b4 to attack his bishop on a6 and also threaten 25.♖xb3. When we see this type of double attack, we often immediately assume that our opponent's options are limited to passive defense (such as exchanging rooks on a3). However, he countered with 24...♘xc5!. I still had an advantage, but it was not as large as before. What is White's best response now? Find three candidate moves and choose the best one.

Discussion

The moves 25.e3 and 25.♗f1 are still good for me. However, I was so surprised by 24...♘xc5 that I impulsively played 25.♖xb3. If you too selected that move, read on! After 25...♘xb3 26.♕d1 (instead of this, 26.♘xa6 would give Black only a small advantage), I was hit with another unexpected shot: 26...♗xd4+!. There followed 27.♗xd4 ♕b4 28.♗b2 ♕c5+ 29.♔h1 ♘xa1 and White was lost.

The lesson here is that when your opponent plays a move like ...♘xc5 that catches you totally off-guard, you must sit on your hands, take a few deep breaths, and not make a move for at least 60 seconds. You simply must allow yourself to calm down ("get sober") because at this moment you have the attention span of a drunk driver on an obstacle course! While sitting on your hands, calmly scan the board for potential candidate moves. Had I followed this rule after Black played 25...♘xb3, it's easy to see that 26.♘xa6 is far better than the losing 26.♕d1.

T43: White to Move

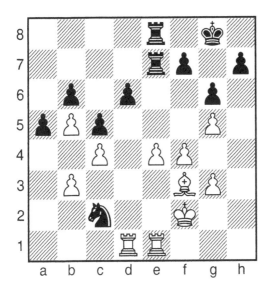

In a 2015 FIDE-rated event at the Marshall Chess Club, I was White in this position against NM Ricardo Perez Billinghurst. Find three candidate moves and choose the best one.

Discussion

I thought that Black was slightly better here because, once he moves his knight to d4, it will be a monster piece that can never be dislodged and attacks my backward b3-pawn. In addition, I can never exchange all the rooks because that knight would dominate my bishop and tie me down to the defense of the b3-pawn.

That thought process led me to consider the idea of *Transforming* the position by playing 33.♖xd6. Had I realized that the position was equal (which it was!), I would have settled for 33.♖e2. But since I thought I was worse, 33.♖xd6 appeared to be a low-risk way of transforming the position and creating complications. That seemed better than being slowly ground down in the endgame. That move must have rattled my opponent, because after 33...♘xe1 34.♔xe1 ♖e6 35.♖d7 ♖8e7 36.♖d8+ ♖e8 37.♖d7 ♖6e7 38.♖d6, he refused to accept the fact that he was only equal and played 38...♖b8?. He then went downhill without much of a fight after 39.e5 ♔f8 40.♗d5 ♔g7 41.♔f2 h6 42.gxh6 ♔xh6 43.♔f3 ♔g7 44.♔e4 ♖a7 45.g4 a4 46.bxa4 ♖xa4 47.♖d7 ♔f8 48.e6 ♖a1 49.♔e5 g5 50.f5, resigning a few moves later.

T44: White to Move

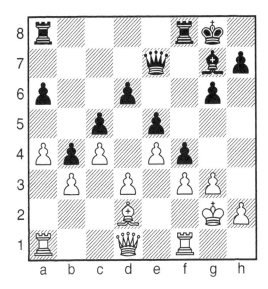

In this position I had White against NM Todd Lunna in a 2015 event in New Jersey. Black has a slight advantage. Find three candidate moves and choose the best one.

Defending Under Pressure

Discussion

The queenside is blocked and Black has a space advantage on the kingside. So the best candidates are 21.♕e2, 21.♖g1, and 21.♖h1. Essentially, these are non-committal waiting moves. They are passive but retain some flexibility for White. However, it was obvious that Black's plan is to advance his g- and h-pawns. So I decided to build a bunker *(Restraint)* by playing 21.g4 to prevent Black from opening the f-file at some point with ...f4xg3. Believe it or not, my move gives Black a definite advantage. The position is now very difficult to hold because White has absolutely no pawn breaks or opportunities to exchange pieces until Black decides when such exchanges will benefit him.

Also, playing 21.g4 eliminates my last source of flexibility. Now Black can build up a huge attack behind the space advantage created by the "spear" pawn on f4. How he converted this advantage into a slow squeeze is a textbook example and worthy of close study:

21.g4 ♗f6 22.♔f2 ♔f7 23.♔e2 ♖h8 24.♖h1 h5 25.h3 ♖h6 26.♕g1 ♖ah8 27.♕g2 ♗h4 28.♗e1 hxg4 29.hxg4 ♕g5 30.♗xh4 ♖xh4 31.♖ag1 ♕h6 32.♖xh4 ♕xh4 33.♔f1 ♔f6 34.♔e2 ♔g5 35.♔f1 a5 36.♔e2 ♕h2 37.♔f1 ♖h3 38.♕xh2 ♖xh2 39.♖g2 ♖h3 40.♔f2 ♔h4 41.♔e2 ♖h1 42.♔f2 ♔h3 0-1

This was a powerful lesson on the danger of passive, inflexible moves that leave you with nothing but "waiting" moves while the opponent builds a winning attack. The danger sign should have been Black's space advantage on the kingside combined with the closed queenside.

T45: White to Move

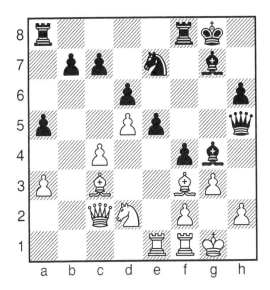

At a 2015 FIDE-rated competition in New York, I was White here against NM Karan Bhatty. Black is better because of his kingside initiative. Find three candidate moves and identify the best one.

Discussion

The obvious candidates are 21.♕d3, 21.♕d1, and 21.♗g4. All seek to hold the position via a *Restraint* approach to dampening Black's initiative. So how do you find the best one? Since this is a fairly fluid situation with likely exchanges, that's a warning sign that you have to switch into calculation mode by looking 2-3 moves deep.

Eager to trade some pieces, I played 21.♕d1, forcing the exchange of at least one piece. That was a superficial assessment since now Black can exchange *two* pieces and increase his advantage: 21.♕d1 ♗xf3 22.♕xf3 ♕xf3 23.♘xf3 b5!.

At the starting position, the "dream" square for my knight was e4. That should have been a clue that I don't want it diverted to the inferior f3 square. The move 21.♕d3 is also poor because it, too, forces my knight to go to f3 after Black captures my bishop there. That leaves 21.♗g4. It's the best move. Then, after 21...♕xg4 22.f3! followed by 23.♘e4, Black still has some advantage, but White is still very much in the game.

The lesson here is that when all the candidate moves appear to be of similar value and there are likely to be two or more exchanges of pawns or pieces within the next few moves, that's a signal that you need to calculate 2-3 moves deep for each of the candidate moves.

T46: Black to Move

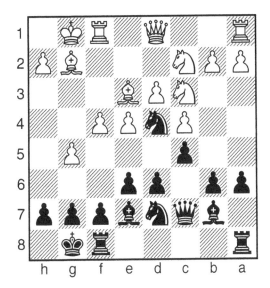

In a 2014 event in New Jersey, I was Black in this position against NM Alexander Crump. Find three candidate moves and choose the best one.

Discussion

The three best choices are 1...b5, 1...♘xc2, and 1...h6. That last one might look weak at first glance, but it's sound if Black knows how to follow it up. A sample line is 1...h6 2.gxh6 ♘xc2 3.♕xc2 g6 4.f5 ♔h7, when White is better but Black is still in the game. Simpler and better is the classic counter-attacking move 1...b5 and White has only a slight advantage. Instead, however, I played 1...e5. Why is this move weak? The answer is that White continues the kingside pawn storm with 2.f5. In addition, Black has now closed access to the e5 square for his knight or dark-squared bishop. Getting one of those pieces to this square would bolster Black's defenses considerably.

T47: Black to Move

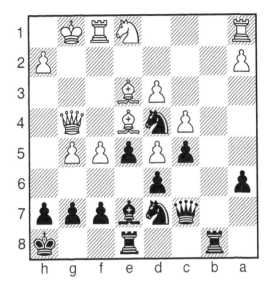

This position occurred several moves later in my game against Alexander Crump. White has increased the pressure on the kingside, but Black still has defensive resources. Find three candidate moves and choose the best one.

Discussion

There are only two good moves here: 1...♖g8 (indirectly preventing White from playing f5-f6 due to ...gxf6 and White's g5-pawn is pinned against his queen!) and 1...f6 (directly preventing White from playing f5-f6 and gaining some space). Instead, I played the passive 1...♗f8. Not only is it passive, but it reduces my defensive resources by blocking my knight from transferring to f8 to bolster my defense of the h7 and g6 squares. After 1...♗f8, White should have played 2.f6 with a completely winning position. A simple question would have warned me of the danger: What purpose does 1...♗f8 serve? There is no obvious purpose, other than aimlessly moving a piece closer to the king. A well-known term for this type of move is "pushing wood."

T48: Black to Move

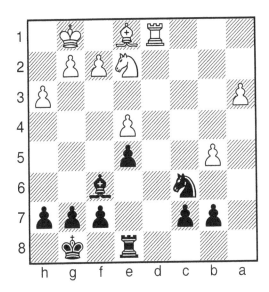

Here's another game where I played Black against IM Jay Bonin. Black has four reasonable candidate moves. Find all four and then choose the best one.

Discussion

The potential moves (ranked from best to worst) are 24...♞d8, 24...♞d4, 24...♖d8, and 24...♞b8. Did you find them all? Why is 24...♞d8 a less risky move than 24...♞d4 ? In the game I chose 24...♞d4. Play then continued 25.♞xd4 exd4 26.f3 ♗e7 27.♗b4! ♗xb4 28.axb4 ♖d8 29.♚f2 ♚f8 30.♚e2 ♖d6 31.♖c1 ♖b6 32.♖c5 and White had a large advantage due to my indefensible pawn on d4. Instead of 24...♞d4 leading to the transfer of my pawn from e5 to d4, 24...♞d8 was a smooth way to regroup my knight to e6, defending the c7-pawn and maintaining a solid central pawn on e5. That would have given Black a fully equal position.

The lesson here is that when we're defending, it's not enough to avoid tactical mistakes in order to hold the position. Any move that triggers a change in the pawn structure needs to be evaluated carefully in terms of the health of the pawn structure once the exchanges occur. Had I done that quick evaluation before playing 24...♞d4, it was easy to see that after the exchange of knights, my d4-pawn would be dangerously weak. The move 24...♞d8 looks like a passive retreat, but this is a only temporary stop en route to e6 where the knight is beautifully centralized, protects my c7-pawn, and the e5-pawn remains well protected and controls important squares such as f4 and d4.

T48 (Supplemental Position 1)

(See diagram next page)

These "backward" regrouping moves are psychologically hard to play when we're defending, but they can save many games for the defender. Look at the games of strong positional grandmasters such as Anatoly Karpov and Michael Adams and you'll see many examples of "backward" redeployments for both offensive and defensive purposes. One of the most famous is Karpov – Spassky, Candidates 1974, where in the following position Karpov played 24.♞b1!. This allows White to play c2-c3, driving away Black's active knight and rerouting the knight (via d2 after the rook moves) over to the kingside. It had no prospects on the queenside because of Black's pawn on c6.

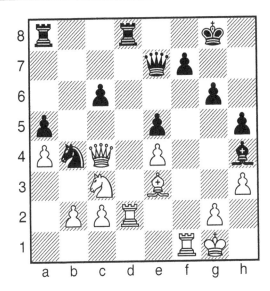

Discussion

After 24.♘b1!, there followed 24...♕b7 25.♔h2 ♔g7 26.c3 ♘a6 27.♖e2 ♖f8 28.♘d2 ♗d8 29.♘f3 and Karpov soon built up a winning attack.

T48 (Supplemental Position 2)

In the final round of the 2018 West Orange (NJ) Chess Club Championship, I was White in this position against NM Peter Radomskyj:

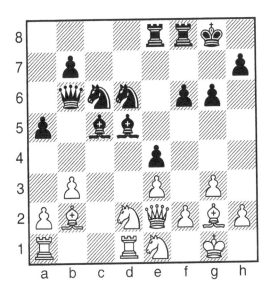

Discussion

It appears that Black is better because of his space advantage and much more active pieces. However, appearances can be deceiving. I was familiar with the Karpov game above and, being a positional player, it took me only 15 seconds to find the "backward attacking move" 21.♘b1! with the threat of a quick ♘c3-a4. This temporary retreat is by far White's best move and gave me a huge advantage (*Stockfish* confirms this assessment). After 21....♘e7 22.♘c3 ♗c6 23.♖ac1 ♗b4 24.♕c2 ♗c3 25.♕c3 ♘d5 26.♕c5 ♕xc5 27.♖xc5, Black is losing material. By winning this game, I became the 2018 club champion.

For one more demonstration of this crucial maneuver, see Position T3, where Black played 35...♘c8!. Take note of where that knight was proudly sitting when my opponent resigned 13 moves later.

T49: White to Move

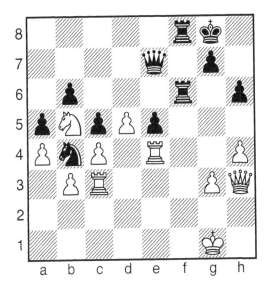

I was White here against NM Arthur Macaspac at a 2016 tournament in New Jersey. Black is about to triple on the f-file and precise play by White is required to hold the balance. Believe it or not, there are only two moves that enable the first player to maintain equality. Find three candidate moves and choose the best one.

Discussion

This is no time for White to get aggressive (A-C-T moves). Instead, he needs to be cautious (P-R-O moves) and find a way to defend against the attack along the f-file. Also, he needs to prevent Black from getting his knight to d4 where it will be a monster piece that supports the queen and rooks (or lead to a passed d-pawn if White trades knights).

36.♕g2 and 36.♖e2 are the only safe moves because they protect White's vulnerable second rank (imagine Black playing the sequence ...♕f7, ...♖f1+, ...♕f2+ and you can see this danger clearly). Instead, I played the superficial counter-attacking move 36.♖ce3 to pressure his e-pawn. This arrangement of the two white rooks reminds me of what the late, legendary chess coach Mark Dvoretsky called "redundant" knights. That occurs when each knight prevents the other one from moving to the square it sits on. This redundancy reduces the knights' mobility. For example, in a position with white knights on d2 and f3, the f3-knight can't move to d2 and the d2-knight can't move to f3.

Applying Dvoretsky's concept to this position, after my last move my rooks are negatively impacted by redundancy. Notice that the e3-rook greatly limits the mobility of the e4-rook. My rook on e4 can't help defend my first and second ranks until the e3-rook gets out of the way! That's why 36.♖e2 was the only non-losing rook move. It would now defend my second rank while the other rook on c3 could move to c1 to defend my first rank. Now the two rooks would be working harmoniously instead of redundantly.

Another problem with my rook move is that it no longer controlled the c2 square, allowing the black knight to escape from its confinement on b4 and jump into the action with 36...♘c2, attacking my rook with tempo on the way to the d4 square. Then I can't play 37.♖e5 since I lose quickly after 37...♖f1+ 38.♕xf1 ♖xf1+ 39.♔xf1 ♘e3+. However, even better would have been 36...♕f7 and White can no longer defend his kingside. Before having your engine show you how hopeless White's position is after 36...♕f7, try to visualize for yourself why that's the case.

So when we feel our opponent's pressure building, we must identify our most vulnerable squares and prevent the opponent from conquering those squares (e.g., in the diagram on the previous page, stopping the black knight from getting to d4 and guarding the weak first and second ranks with either ♕h3-g2 or ♖e4-e2). Then, those defenders will be positioned to exchange some of the opposing pieces, weakening the attack. Also, when deciding where to place those defending pieces, we must ensure that they are coordinating with one another, rather than blocking each other.

Therefore, when our opponent has tripled his major pieces on a file to build an attack, in most cases the best defensive setup is to avoid placing our rooks on the same file (vertical redundancy) or on the same rank (horizontal redundancy). That way, they are controlling different squares rather than some of the same (redundant) squares. In this example after I played ♖ce3, the redundant squares are e2 and e1.

(This page intentionally left blank)

T50: White to Move

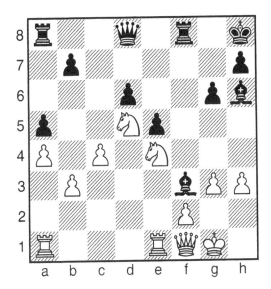

I was playing White here against IM Mikhail Zlotnikov in the 2016 West Orange (NJ) Chess Club Championship. Black is more active based on his bishop pair and pressure on the f-file. However, White's knights are spectacular and his pawn structure is much better. So he has excellent long-term winning chances once he finds a way to eliminate Black's temporary pressure. Find three candidate moves and choose the best one.

Discussion

What stands out in this position is the "lonely" rook on a1. It needs to join the rest of the team, but is limited by the raking black bishops controlling the c1 and d1 squares. So patience is required. Since there are no immediate threats, White has time to use a few moves to shift the rook to an active position. I played 26.♖a2! (the best move) with the idea of "walking up a 4-step staircase" (♖a2-♖c2-♖c3-♖d3). Once on d3, the rook puts pressure on Black's backward d6-pawn and helps defend my kingside. While other moves were good too (e.g., 26.♕d3), further delay in activating the rook could become dangerous.

This is an interesting case of combining *Restraint* (the rook on d3 helps defend my kingside and restrains Black's activity) with *Counter-Attack* (the rook pressures Black's backward pawn on d6). Once I neutralized Black's temporary activity, my structural advantages (a much better pawn structure and a dominant knight on d5) increased significantly and I went on to win this game.

T51: White to Move

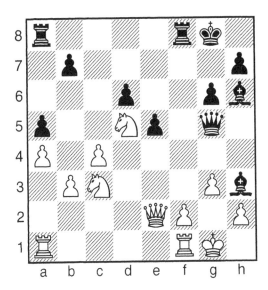

A few moves earlier in my game against Zlotnikov, he played 21...♗h3 attacking my rook. Find three candidate moves and decide which is the best one.

Discussion

There are three good candidate moves for White here: 22.♖fe1, 22.♖fd1, and 22.♘e4. Those last two moves probably surprised you since they both appear to lose the exchange (e.g., 22.♖fd1 allows Black to play 22...♗g4, while 22.♘e4 allows the desperado 22...♗xf1 attacking my queen). I played the cautious 22.♖fe1. Now that you know that the other two candidate moves intentionally "allow" Black to win the exchange, take a moment to visualize the board after each of those exchange-winning moves. Then ask yourself: Why did White permit this and what benefit does he get from it?

Those exchange-dropping moves provide clear-cut examples of *Transformation*. In exchange for a small amount of material, White has eliminated Black's strong light-squared bishop (along with Black's bishop pair); has iron-clad control over the light squares in the center of the board; and has a monster knight on d5 that can never be challenged by Black. For the rest of the game, it dominated Black's "bad" dark-squared bishop.

These positional transformation moves that involve a small sacrifice of material are hard for many players to see. Or else they lack the confidence to play them. Recall a similar transformation in Position T32, where I sacrificed the exchange instead of moving my attacked rook and then having to defend passively against a national master. That transformation was objectively a sound decision, but it had the added benefit of throwing my opponent off-balance. After that, he went on to lose without putting up much resistance.

So while sacrificing the exchange was not essential in this position for White to maintain a small advantage, this is a great training exercise for enhancing your awareness of these transformative moves since there will be many cases where this approach is the only way to save your position when your opponent has a strong initiative or an attack.

T52: Black to Move

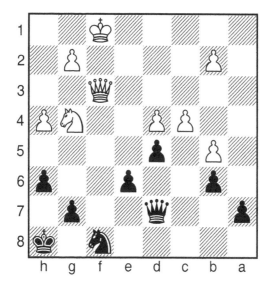

A typical comment by grandmasters in their game annotations is something along the lines of, "the position here is roughly equal, but it's much easier for me to play, so I refused my opponent's offer of a draw." In this position I was Black against the late NM Boris Privman (2340 at the time of the game). The game is roughly equal, but White's position is much easier to play because of his more active pieces and space advantage. So while *Stockfish* evaluates the position as equal, Black needs to tread carefully to avoid slipping into a losing position, especially against an exceptional endgame player like Privman. Find three candidate moves and choose the best one.

Discussion

The best candidates are 40...♔g8, 40...♕e8, 40...♕c8, and 40...♕e7. This last one requires some calculation since it allows White to play 41.cxd5, seemingly winning a pawn. While all are sound choices, 40...♕c8 is the best one because it serves a dual purpose: It protects my f8-knight and threatens a pawn capture with check on c4. So it combines *Restraint* with *Counter-Attack*. White can't then win a pawn with 41.cxd5 because after Black recaptures with 41...exd5, Black's queen threatens ...♕c1+ and also attacks White's knight on g4!

Recall the rule of thumb here: When a move is likely to trigger one or more exchanges (like 40...♕c8 in this example), that's the signal that you *must* calculate each variation at least 2-3 moves deep.

In this position I played 40...♘g6, a positional blunder. White could have continued 41.h5 ♘e7 42.♕f8+ ♔h7 43.♘e5 with a winning advantage. However, his position was so good that even after 41.h5 ♘e7 42.♘e5 ♕e8 43.♘f7+ ♔g8 44.♘d6 ♕f8 45.c5, his advantage was also decisive. The lesson here is that you have to ask yourself if a defensive move has a purpose beyond just saving a piece from being captured, or will that piece be subjected to further harassment after the move. Because my knight was undefended, I instinctively moved it. I did not visualize that, after moving it to g6, White could simply kick it away with 41.h5, driving it to a passive square and allowing White to infiltrate with his queen and knight. Even though I didn't see the counter-attacking idea 40...♕c8, common sense should have led me to move my king to g8 where it protects both my knight *and* the f7 square.

Let's be honest – when our emotions are not heightened and we have sufficient energy, it's easy to find simple moves like 40...♔g8. After the game is over, we wonder how we could have overlooked such a simple defense! So when you're not feeling level-headed or your energy is low, you are less able to play by instinct (i.e., quickly seeing the best move and playing it like most of the moves that grandmasters make in blitz games). Instead, you must force yourself to quickly scan for three candidate moves to turn the position into a "multiple-choice test." You can't see the advantages of a move like 40...♕c8 unless it's one of your candidate moves. Playing by instinct when defending under pressure almost always fails.

Note that 40...♘g6 was not a "blunder" in the literal sense of the word since I didn't hang any material. But it was a positional blunder that destroyed the coordination of my knight and queen while allowing White to infiltrate. So while it's crucial not to hang material when defending, that's not enough. We also need to coordinate our pieces, avoid moves that save an attacked piece but have no other purpose (e.g., 40...♘g6), and be on the lookout for opportunities to play active moves (like 40...♕c8 in this position).

(This page intentionally left blank)

T53: White to Move

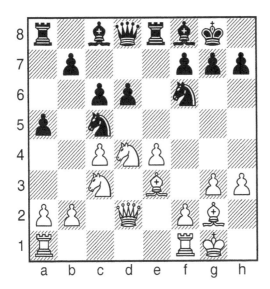

I was White in this game against the expert Shawn Swindell (USCF 2100) at the 2014 U.S. Amateur Team Championship. Find three candidate moves and choose the best one.

Discussion

Black has pressure on my e4-pawn, so I need to take time out from pursuing offensive objectives until I address that issue. Therefore, reasonable candidates include 13.f3, 13.♕c2, and 13.♗g5. I immediately rejected 13.f3 because then Black can fully equalize with 13...d5. I also rejected 13.♕c2 because I thought that after 13...♕e7, I couldn't defend my e4-pawn in view of the fact 14.f3 is no longer possible since my e3-bishop is now unprotected, allowing Black to strike with 14...d5!. So I chose the inferior 13.♗g5, allowing Black to win the bishop pair with 13...h6.

However, since the natural move in this position was 13.♕c2, I should have looked more closely to see if Black's threats after 13...♕e7 were "real." Turns out they're a mirage: after 13.♕c2! ♕e7, White calmly plays 14.♖fe1. Then neither black knight can capture my e4-pawn: 14...♘cxe4 15.♗f4! wins for White, as does 14...♘fxe4 15.♘xc6! bxc6 16.♗xc5 dxc5 17.♗e4 with a double attack (18.♗h7+ winning Black's queen and 18.♗c6 winning the exchange).

The visual cue that should have tipped me off that Black's threats were probably not real is the position of the black queen after it moves to e7. Rarely can a series of captures successfully be played with the queen leading the charge. The reason is that it's too exposed. I call the proper defensive technique in these cases "loading the gun." In this position, I did not have to defend the pawn directly. By "loading the gun" with 14.♖fe1, I could have waited for the intruders (the black knights) to attempt to steal my pawn on e4. My gun would be waiting for them! The beauty of the moves 13.♕c2 and 14.♖fe1 is that they not only defend against Black's pressure on my e4-pawn, but they're also natural developing moves, so these pieces are well placed for offensive operations.

T54: White to Move

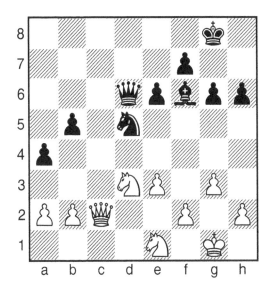

I played White here against NM Boris Feldman (no relation to Yevgeny Feldman) in a 2011 Marshall Chess Club weekend event. This is another one of those positions that are objectively equal but much easier to play for one side (in this example, Black has the easier game).

Black's knight is well placed on d5, so a natural candidate move for White is e3-e4 to drive it to a less active square or force an exchange. Evaluate this move to determine if it's poor, reasonable, or strong.

Discussion

When I played 1.e4, I was almost certain that Black would reply with 1...
♘b4. I welcomed that exchange because it trades his active knight on d5
for my more passive one on d3. Also, this eliminates the "redundancy" of
my two knights (e.g., my d3-knight prevented my e1-knight from moving
to d3; see our discussion of redundancy in Position T38). So I immediately
captured his knight with 2.♘xb4. So far so good, since 1.e4 is not really a
mistake as long as White follows up accurately. However, by immediately
capturing his knight, his queen recaptures with 2...♕xb4 and now has a
double attack on my b2-pawn and my e1-knight. So instead of the losing
move 2.♘xb4, White needs to find the non-obvious 2.♕e2!, when the
position is roughly equal.

The lesson here is never to make "automatic captures," especially those
we were expecting (or planning) a move or two earlier. Emotionally, it's
hard to resist capturing the black b4-knight when it's attacking my queen
since my objective in playing e3-e4 was to drive the knight to that square
so I could exchange it! So when you have decided to play a multi-move
sequence (e.g., e3-e4 followed by capturing on b4), you must stop the
action after each move to briefly visualize the position that will be on
the board at that moment. In this example, it's not hard to see that after
the black queen recaptures on b4, it has a double attack on b2 and e1.
This does not require any deep calculation. Rather, it's taking the time to
"see" (Freeze Frame) the position on the board so that the image is firmly
in your mind. I didn't "see" the negative consequences of capturing his
knight on b4 because I had already made up my mind a move earlier to
make that capture.

T55: White to Move

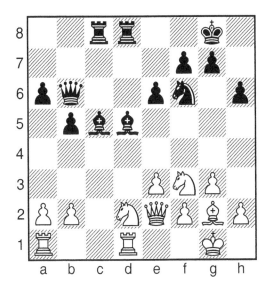

This was earlier in my game against Boris Feldman (see T54). The position is equal but easier for Black to play. So White needs to be cautious to avoid drifting into an inferior position. Identify three candidate moves and choose the best one.

Discussion

White has no active possibilities, so the priority is to find ways to neutralize Black's more-active pieces through exchanges. The best moves to achieve this are ♘e1 and ♘e5. Both force the exchange of the light-squared bishops and ease White's defense.

I'm sure that some readers chose the "active" e3-e4, forcing Black's bishop to retreat and grabbing some space in the center. However, that gives Black a sizable advantage. With a symmetrical pawn structure, White has no attacking chances. So instead of grabbing space, moving the pawn to e4 just loosens White's position and creates concrete targets for Black (i.e., the pawns on e4 and f2).

Therefore, I played the solid retreat ♘e1. You're aware of the value of these backward knight moves from my commentary in Position T48. That move forced the exchange of bishops and gave me a fully equal game.

T56: Black to Move

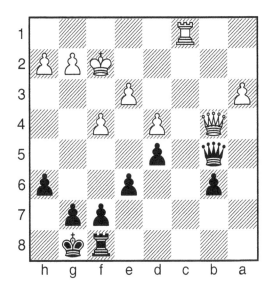

I was Black here against NM Yevgeny Feldman at a Marshall Chess Club event. Find three candidate moves and select the best one.

Discussion

Here again we have a position that is objectively equal but much easier for one player (White) to play. White's rook is on an open file and Black's queen must move somewhere, thereby delaying the activation of the f8-rook for at least one more move. So Black has to be very careful. Three moves come to mind: 30...♛xb4, 30...♛d3, and 30...♛a6. Since I knew that I was playing for no more than a draw, it made sense to consider trading queens since that creates a completely symmetrical pawn structure and closes access to the queenside by White's king after 30...♛xb4 31.axb4 b5. Now my rook can easily defend my b5-pawn.

However, that whole line of reasoning was wrong. What I failed to consider is that after 31...b5, White ignores my b-pawn and plays 32.♖c7. Now while my rook will be sitting on the queenside passively, White's rook and king will team up for a decisive breakthrough against the "symmetrical" pawn structure on the other side of the board. So after 32...♖b8 33.f5 ♖b6 34.fxe6 fxe6 35.♔f3 ♔h7 36.♔f4 ♔g6 37.♔e5, White had a winning advantage.

T57: Black to Move

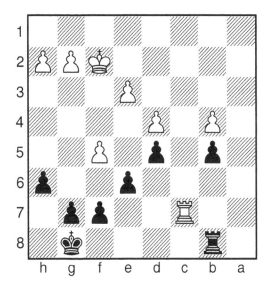

Now that you know that 33...罝b6 was a poor move for Black in the last position, you have a chance to do better than I did during the game. First answer this question: Why was 33...罝b6 a bad move? Then find three candidate moves and choose the best one.

Discussion

The only move to stay in the game is 33...exf5. That will not be the first choice for most players since it isolates Black's d-pawn, thereby creating another target for the white rook. However, it is essential since if White is allowed to exchange pawns on e6, Black's king is trapped on the back rank, allowing the white monarch to march up the board as occurred in the game. That is why 33...♖b6 was a bad move: It allowed the exchange of the f-pawn.

So Black needs to bite the bullet and play ...exf5 to maintain a pawn on f7. That would allow Black to activate his king by playing ...g7-g6 followed by ...♔g7 or ...♔f8 instead of remaining imprisoned on the first rank or taking the long detour via h7-g6. Best play after 33...exf5 is 34.♖c5 g6 35.♖d5 ♔f8. White is still better, but Black is hanging on and has drawing chances.

The lesson here is that sometimes when defending we need to play anti-positional moves that provide active play (e.g., ...exf5 in this position) to ensure that we don't drift into a totally passive position. This is especially true in rook endgames, where activity often fully compensates for defects in our pawn structure or when we're down a pawn.

T58: White to Move

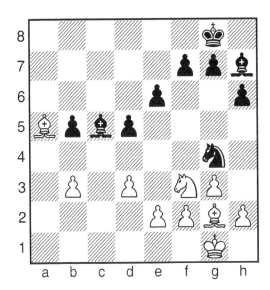

I had White in this position against IM Larry Kaufman at the 2008 U.S. Amateur Team Championship. He achieved the grandmaster title the following year after winning the World Senior Championship. Black has just played 24...♗c5. What is White's best move?

Discussion

I have the advantage because of Black's inactive bishop on h7. However, he's attacking my f2-pawn. A natural move would be 25.d4 to stop the attack and gain space in the center. However, that allows Black to equalize immediately since it frees his light-squared bishop. There appears to be no other way to defend my pawn. Then I noticed a simple counter-attacking move that allows me to maintain my advantage: 25.h3!. This is a good calculation exercise for you: Why must Black retreat his knight instead of capturing the f2-pawn with either the knight or the bishop?

After the forced 25...♘f6, I found a beautiful four-move "knight tour" that won the b5-pawn by force: 26.b4! ♗a7 27.♘e5 ♗d4 28.♘c6 ♗c3 29.♘a7 ♗d2 30.♘xb5. Black's bishop is still trapped on h7 and I have an extra (and passed) pawn on the queenside. I went on to win this memorable game. The rest of the game went:

30...♔f8 31.♘a3 ♔e8 32.♘b1 ♗c1 33.♔f1 ♔d7 34.♔e1 ♘e8 35.♔d1 ♗b2 36.♔c2 ♗d4 37.e3 ♗a7 38.♗f3 ♘d6 39.♔d2 ♘b7 40.♗d1 ♘xa5 41.bxa5 ♔c6 42.♗a4+ ♔b7 43.♗b5 ♗b8 44.♔c3 ♗c7 45.♔b4 ♗d6+ 46.♔a4 g5 47.♘d2 ♗f5 48.g4 ♗g6 49.♘f3 e5 50.h4 e4 51.h5 ♗xh5 52.gxh5 exf3 53.♗d7 ♗h2 54.♗g4 ♗g1 55.♗xf3 ♔c6 56.e4 ♗xf2 57.exd5+ ♔d6 58.♔b5 f5 59.♔c4 ♗a7 60.d4 ♗b8 61.♗d1 ♗c7 62.a6 ♗b6 63.♗c2 f4 64.♗d1 ♗a7 65.♗f3 ♗b6 66.♔d3 g4 67.♗xg4 ♔xd5 68.♗f3+ ♔d6 69.♔e4 ♗a7 70.d5 ♗e3 71.♔f5 ♔e7 72.♔g6 ♗c5 73.♔xh6 ♔f6 74.♔h7 ♔f7 75.h6 ♗b6 76.♗h5+ ♔f8 77.♔g6 ♔g8 78.d6 **1-0**

Notice that Black's bishop remained imprisoned on the kingside until move 51, when he exchanged it with 51...♗xh5. He then had an equal game for the next 15 moves until he made a subtle, non-obvious mistake with 65...♗b6 which blocked his king from mounting a quick attack on my passed pawn on a6.

T59: Black to Move

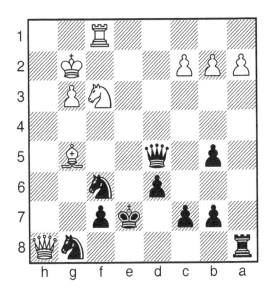

This position was reached in the game Lange – Anderssen, Berlin 1852, after White's 24.♗g5. Find three candidate moves for Black and choose the best one.

Discussion

It appears that Black is about to lose a piece due to the threat of ♖e1+ followed by ♗xf6. Anderssen was unable to find a saving move and resigned! So clearly this is an *Only Move* position. Recall from my commentary on Carlsen–Topalov (Position T6) regarding "Only Move" situations: You must look at *every* reasonable move.

So try that right now for practice: List *every* (reasonable) move for Black here. Obviously none of the pawn moves on the queenside qualifies as "reasonable" since they do nothing to stop White's deadly threats. Here's the list: ...♖f8, ...♖e8, ...♖d8, ...♕f5, ...♕c4, ...♕c5. While you're at it, explain why a move by the black rook to any square on the a-file is bad.

Now that you have the list, it's obvious that White is planning ♖e1. So that should be a huge clue in helping you to eliminate most of the losing moves. For example, if Black plays 24...♔d7 to avoid the rook check on e1, White captures the knight with 25.♗f6 and the knight can't recapture the bishop because White's queen will capture the rook on a8. Why does 24...♖e8 fail? Because White replies 25.♖e1+ ♔d7 26.♖xe8 ♔xe8 27.♗xf6 and the knight can't retake on f6 since it's pinned by the white queen.

What about 24...♕f5 ? Does that work? Yes! Then after 25.♖e1+ ♔d7, Black is better! He has protected his f6-knight and threatens 26...♕xc2+. Now that you see it, it probably doesn't seem that difficult. But unless we list all the reasonable moves and then eliminate them one by one, it's almost impossible to find these types of "only" defensive moves.

T60: Black to Move

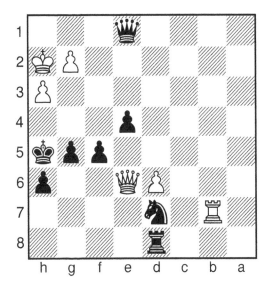

Find three candidate moves for Black and name the best one.

Discussion

This position was reached in Grischuk – Vaganian, Mainz (active) 2004. Actually, Black resigned before White had the chance to play 52.♕xf5. So this is clearly an *Only Move* situation. Therefore, list every reasonable candidate move for Black and then use the method described in the last position to find the only saving move.

Only 51...♘e5 saves Black. It provides some temporary defense for his king. Since White is a piece down, he has little choice but to take the knight with 52.♕xe5. On e5, the queen is much less dangerous for Black than on f5. So the knight move to e5 is a diversionary tactic to buy time for Black to move his queen to a more active square.

However, after White captures the knight, again Black is faced with an *Only Move* situation! So now list every reasonable move here. The solution is 52...♕d2!, with the double threat of 53...♕f4+ and 53...♕xd6.

Listing every reasonable move instead of diving into the first move that captures your attention is the only way to find these magical defensive moves (unless you pick the right move by luck).

T61: Black to Move

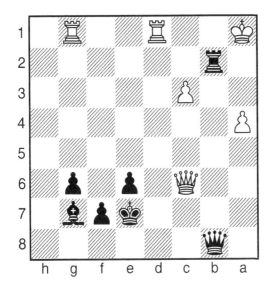

In a 2014 event in New Jersey, I was Black here against Aaron Jacobson (rated 2180 at the time and now above 2400). He's the brother of GM Brandon Jacobson, who appeared earlier in this book (see T4). Find three candidate moves for Black and choose the best one.

Discussion

Obviously Black needs to look for an active move before his opponent has a chance to use his superior force to attack the exposed black king. Moving my rook so I can threaten ...♗xc3+ seems necessary. If you came to the same conclusion, you probably boiled down the candidate moves to 32...♖c2 and 32...♖b3. Yes, one of them gives Black an equal game and the other one loses! Now comes the hard part: Spend some time figuring out which is which!

If you've absorbed the lessons contained in previous positions, you'll note that one of these rook moves is more active than the other. Also, one of them eliminates the "redundancy" relationship between Black's queen and rook (the rook on the b-file partially blocks the queen's path on that file). So those criteria would have been enough to indicate that 32...♖c2 is probably better than 32...♖b3. Now the rook and the queen complement each other since they *both* attack the b2 square. Notice also how a rook on c2 (instead of b3) jointly controls the h2 square with the queen on b8.

You might ask how that square can possibly be relevant in this razor-sharp position where all the action is on the queenside. Well, the rook move to b3 allows a long forced mate starting with 33.♖d7+ ♔f8 34.♖xf7+ ♔xf7 35.♕d7+ ♔f6 36.♖f1+ ♔g5 37.♕e7+ ♔g4 38.♕xe6+, etc. Had the rook instead moved to c2, then this sequence of checks no longer leads to mate because Black can play 37...♔h5. Then 38.♖h1+ is met by 38...♖h2!. Amazing how that square is relevant after all! White missed that spectacular mate and the game ended in a draw a few moves later.

While that was a beautiful mating attack, you did *not* need to see it to choose 32...♖c2 instead of 32...♖b3. The thinking process of comparing the two moves using the criteria of maximizing piece mobility and improving cooperation between the queen and the rook by eliminating their redundancy on the b-file would have been enough to choose correctly. This is not to say that logical thought processes will always lead to the best move. However, they significantly increase the odds of success when we're short on time, have low energy, and/or lack the calculating ability needed to find the best move based on an exhaustive analysis of the position. That's exactly when we need the types of thinking techniques covered in this book.

T62: Black to Move

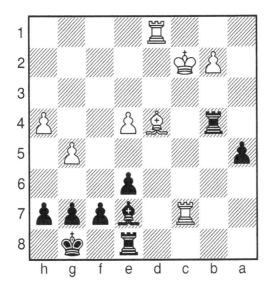

I had Black here against NM Matthew O'Brien in a 2016 event in New Jersey. I have an advantage due to my extra pawn, but White's pieces are more active and I need to watch out for back-rank mate threats since there is no easy way to provide a flight square for my king. That means I need to be defensive-minded for the time being. Find three candidate moves and choose the best one.

Discussion

There are three reasonable moves: 31...♗f8, 31...♗d6, and 31...♔f8. Even after 15 minutes of analysis, *Stockfish* evaluates 31...♗f8 as better than the other two. The alternative 31...♔f8 partially addresses the back-rank issue and also appears to protect the bishop, allowing my rook to move to a more active square. However, after my rook moves (e.g., 32...♖eb8), I need to watch out for such tactics as 33.♗g7+ ♔g7 34.♖xe7. Or 33.♖xe7 ♔xe7 34.♗c5+. So while 31...♔f8 is a solid move, it puts more demands on your tactical alertness. The guideline in these cases is that if you're low on energy or short on time and you have two moves (e.g., ...♔f8 and ...♗f8) that appear of equal value, you should select the more cautious one.

The third choice, 31...♗d6, is solid too and attacks White's c7-rook. However, what is the planned follow-up? Also, it does not help Black solve the issue of his vulnerable back rank.

The move 31...♗f8 is best since it serves multiple purposes:

- The bishop is better protected than after 31...♔f8, allowing the e8-rook more freedom of movement;
- The e8-rook is now activated (e.g., it supports the threat 32...e5 followed by the capture of the e4-pawn after White moves the bishop);
- It doesn't fully solve the back-rank issue, but does provide partial protection against mate until a permanent solution is found.

So this move is a combination of *Prevention* and *Activity*. If you chose 31...♗d6 but did not consider 31...♗f8 at all, you get credit for preferring a solid move that is only slightly worse than 31...♗f8. However, the point of many of the exercises in this book is to widen your thought process to be on the lookout for the types of moves (e.g., the "backward" move ...♗e7-f8) that you normally do not consider. That's because there will be many situations where that type of move *will* be the only good one in the position. These training exercises enhance your pattern recognition so that you'll have access to these patterns during your tournament games. By the end of the book, what matters is how much you've learned that you can apply in your own play, not how many you got "right."

T63: White to Move

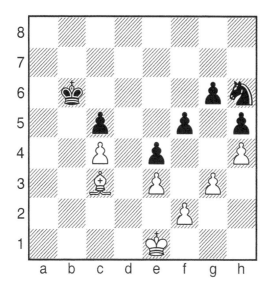

In this position, I was White against NM Yefim Treger at the 2000 New Jersey State Championship. Evaluate these three candidate moves and choose the best one: 78.♔d1, 78.♔e2, and 78.♗b2.

Discussion

This is another position that is fully equal but much easier for one side to play. Black's knight is more mobile than my "bad" bishop, so there is the potential to drift into a lost endgame if White is not careful. A perfect example of this is the line 78.♗b2? ♘f7 79.♔d2 ♘d6 80.♔c3 ♘b7 81.♔b3 ♘a5+ 82.♔c3 ♘c6 83.♗a1 ♘e5, when Black will win either the c4- or the f2-pawn!

I played 78.♔e2. My thought process went as follows: "I need to activate my king. The moves ♔d1 and ♔d2 don't meet that objective since Black can play ...♘g4, attacking my f2-pawn and forcing my king to return to e1 or move to e2. Therefore, I'll just move it to e2 immediately." Seems like a well-reasoned move, right? Yes, it was logical – *assuming* that Black did indeed play ...♘g4. However, it's a losing move because I overlooked the danger to my c4-pawn. After 78.♔e2, it now requires *three* moves for me to defend that pawn (two king moves and one move by the bishop). However, Black can attack it within *two* moves (...♘f7-d6).

In hindsight, the weakness of my c4-pawn is completely obvious. I was so focused on my vulnerable f2-pawn that I forgot to protect the c4-pawn on the other side of the board. There are no active moves available to White. That should be the warning signal that he must carefully look for cautious *(Prevention* or *Restraint)* moves. Among the three candidate moves above, only 78.♔d1 maintains equality. The king is now ready to quickly protect the c4-pawn while staying close to the f2-pawn.

In endings featuring a knight against a bad bishop with pawns on both sides of the board, the potential for mistakes like this is high. So adopting an "any move draws" mentality is dangerous. In such positions, the knight's potential to reach all 64 squares on the board should heighten the defender's sense of danger. That means you have to focus deeply on finding *Prevention* moves and actively scan for ways that this prancing knight can attack targets on *both* sides of the board.

T64: White to Move

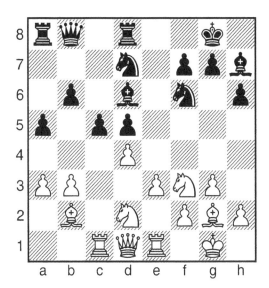

In a 2000 event at the Marshall Chess Club, I was White in this position against the late Ilye Figler, a very strong master then rated 2370. Find three candidate moves and pick the best one.

Discussion

While the position is fully equal, Black's game is easier to play due to his more active pieces and space advantage. White's advantages are his solid structure and excellent "hypermodern" pressure with the fianchettoed bishops (e.g., at some point Black is likely to wind up with an isolated pawn on d5 or hanging pawns on d5 and c5 after White plays dxc5).

While there are at least four good moves here (18.a4, 18.♗c3, 18.♘h4, and 18.♘b1), I want to focus on the last one since it is not the type of "backward" move that most players below the master level consider. Also, *Stockfish* rates it as slightly better than the other three moves.

From my prior commentary in Position T48 about backward knight moves and in Position T49 about "redundant knights," why do you think 18.♘b1 is a good move? For starters, it reroutes the knight to a more active square (i.e., it was passive due to Black's d5-pawn). Then it's ready to move to c3 where it puts pressure on Black's d5-pawn and controls the a4 and b5 squares. It fits the old saying, "sometimes you need to take one step back to go two steps forward." Also, it eliminates the redundancy between White's two knights since now the f3-knight has access to the d2 square. Redundant knights are usually not a problem when this is a temporary state of affairs, but that redundancy should be eliminated at the first available opportunity.

Instead, I played the careless 18.♕e2. Take a moment to see why that move is poor. The answer is that now Black played 18...a4!, damaging my queenside pawn structure while opening the a-file for his rook. Had the queen remained on d1, 18...a4 would have involved a pawn sacrifice since I could play 19.bxa4.

So the "backward" move 18.♘b1 is actually an *Activity* move since b1 is not the primary destination for this knight. Instead, it's a "transit square" on the way to a much more active location. It's a clone of 21.♘b1 in T48 Supplemental Position 2.

T65: Black to Move

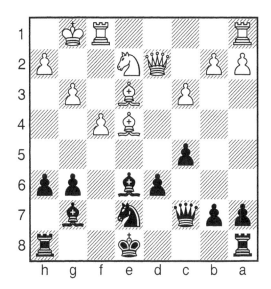

In a 2000 event at the Marshall Chess Club, I was Black here against the 2330-rated master Whee Ky Ma . The position is equal but easier to play for White because he's fully developed and I haven't castled yet. Evaluate these three moves and choose the best one: 16...♗f5, 16...0-0, or 16...♘f5.

Discussion

Improving at chess requires not only the ability to spot good moves, but also the ability to eliminate seemingly good moves that contain a flaw. Here the move 16...♘f5 looks perfectly reasonable, as it threatens to win the bishop pair or force the e3-bishop to retreat to the passive f2 square. That's a reasonable thought process up to a point. However, it fails to account for White's aggressive intentions with a kingside pawn storm. So moving the knight to f5 gave White the chance to accelerate his attack with 17.g4!. Then, after 17...♘xe3 18.♕xe3, White would have been much better. With Black's knight gone from the board, his g6-pawn is extremely weak and the king is still vulnerable. White missed this opportunity and played the passive 17.♗f2, restoring equality. That leads us to the next position.

T66: Black to Move

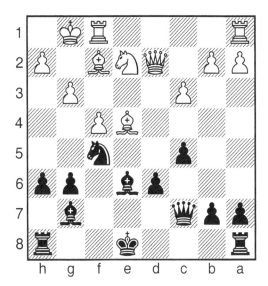

Recall that White has just played the passive 17.♗f2. What is Black's best move in this position? Find three candidate moves before reading the commentary on the next page.

Discussion

Actually, there are only two good moves here: 17...0-0-0 to get the king to a safer place and connecting the rooks, and 17...h5 to stabilize the position of the knight on f5. *Stockfish* considers castling to be slightly better than 17...h5, but both moves give Black full equality. Castling short (17...0-0) would have been weaker because now the black king is facing a white pawn storm starting with 18.g4.

T67: Black to Move

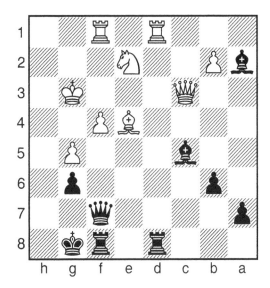

Later in the game against Whee Ky Ma, we reached this position with Black to play. Who do you think is better and why? Find three candidate moves for Black and choose the best one.

153

Discussion

White is slightly better here because of his more active and better co-ordinated pieces. White has pressure on my g6-pawn and could increase this pressure with moves like ♕c3-c2. So Black has to be careful to avoid slipping into a losing position. Therefore, I needed to be looking for cautious *(Prevention* and *Restraint)* moves and wait until later to seek potential counter-attacking opportunities against his insecure king and backward pawn on f4.

That line of thinking suggests two potential moves: 35...♕g7 to seek an exchange of queens, and 35...♖xd1 to trade a pair of rooks. I didn't see the danger and played 35...♖de8. Amazingly, that seemingly solid move gives White a winning advantage after 36.♖h1 (threatening mate) 36...♕g7 37.♕c2. He's now threatening 38.♖h6 and my kingside is collapsing. Talk about a lightning bolt seemingly out of nowhere!

Had I played 35...♖xd1, White would no longer have had a decisive invasion on the kingside: 36.♖xd1 ♖e8 37.♖h1 ♕g7 38.♕c2 ♗f7 39.♖h6 ♖e6! and the position is equal. Those two variations look very similar. The difference is one tempo. By exchanging rooks on d1 in the second variation, Black gains the time needed to reposition his pieces to defend his kingside. You may have hesitated to exchange the rooks on d1 because you didn't want to give White's other rook control of the open d-file. However, then Black plays ...♖f8-e8 and controls the open e-file while targeting the e4-bishop and the e2-knight.

T68: Black to Move

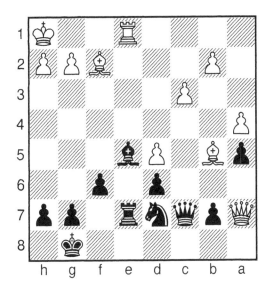

I'm Black here against NM Mark Kernighan in a 2015 tournament in New Jersey. This was the third game of the day, so I was very tired. When our energy is low, we tend to see "phantom" threats because our ability to calculate quickly and accurately is diminished. Find three candidate moves and select the best one.

Discussion

There are a few good moves here, such as 34...f5, 34...♔f7, 34...♔f8, and 34...♖f7. I was about to play 34...♔f7 (the best move), but then noticed that White has the "threat" of 35.♗xd7 ♖xd7 36.♗b6 with a double attack on my queen and a5-pawn. So I met that threat by playing 34...♘c5, not realizing that I was leaving my back rank vulnerable to a winning invasion: 35.♕a8+ ♔f7 36.♕h8 h6 37.♗e2. White has a decisive attack while my knight and queen are passively sitting on the other side of the board, unable to come to the defense of my king. Like Position T67, this is another lightning bolt that seemed to come out of nowhere.

What I overlooked after White plays 36.♗b6 was the simple counterattack 36...♕c4 with a double attack against the d5- and a4-pawns. That would give me a large advantage. I didn't really "overlook" it – I never considered *any* moves after I saw that he could play 36.♗b6. I rejected the entire line once I saw that phantom threat.

The lesson here is that when you see a tactical threat by your opponent to win a pawn, the first question you should ask yourself is: Do I have any potential counter-threats at any point during the tactical sequence or after my opponent takes the pawn? Let's be honest, the amount of calculation required by Black in this position is very little. Seeing and then defending against these phantom threats is controlled by the emotional centers of our brain (e.g., the amygdala) that are highly attuned to danger.

These emotions can hijack the logical part of our brain (the frontal cortex), causing us to react quickly to avert the danger. Therefore, anytime we "see" these tactical threats, our first order of business is to take a few deep breaths to decrease the "fear factor." That will allow the logical part of the brain to objectively evaluate the threat and sometimes "allow" the opponent to carry out their threat.

T69: Black to Move

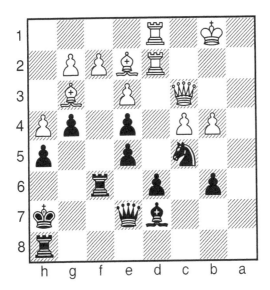

Here is another tournament game where I was Black against Mark Kernighan. Evaluate these four moves and choose the best one: 37...♘a4, 37...♘b7, 37...♘a6, and 37...♘d3.

Discussion

Believe it or not, this is an *Only Move* position. Just one move (37... ♘d3) gives Black equality. The other three choices (and all other moves) are losing! Now that you know this, take a close look at 37...♘a4, 37... ♘a6, and 37...♘b7 and determine why they are bad. Also, come up with an explanation for why 37...♘d3 leads to an equal position.

After 37...♘a4, one winning line is 38.♕e5! dxe5 39.♖d7 ♖e8 40.♔c2 ♔g6 41.♖xe7 ♖xe7 42.♔b3 and White's advantage is huge. After 37... ♘b7, 38.♗xe5! wins; while after 37...♘a6, the simple 38.c5, attacking the undefended a6-knight and breaking open the center, gives White a crushing position.

After 37...♘d3 38.♗xd3 exd3 39.♕xd3+ ♗f5 e4 ♗g6, Black is fully equal. What is his compensation for being a pawn down? White's king is not secure because of his advanced c4- and b4-pawns. In contrast, Black's king is much safer. Also, Black has pressure on the semi-open f-file and White's bishop is very passive on g3. The only way to activate this bishop is by playing f2-f3 at some point, but that allows multiple pawn exchanges that will leave White with an isolated pawn on e3.

The clues to White's tactical threats in this position are his doubled rooks on the queen file and the combined pressure on the e5-pawn by White's queen and dark-squared bishop.

This position provides a powerful lesson on the importance of considering moves that give up a pawn, but provide full dynamic compensation by alleviating the pressure on our position, increasing the activity of our pieces, and providing counter-attacking possibilities. Even if White did not have all those winning tactics in this situation, 37...♘d3 – intentionally sacrificing a pawn – should be given serious consideration. So even if 37...♘b7 did not lose any material, it would have been a poor choice that allowed White to increase his initiative.

I've said it several times so far in this book: Playing passively against stronger players who have the initiative almost always fails. Recall in Position T43 how my master-level opponent, who had the initiative, lost his bearings when I "let" him win the exchange. That completely changed the dynamics of the position and had the added benefit of being objectively sound.

T70: Black to Move

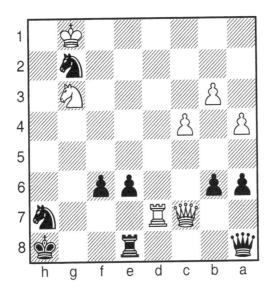

This position was reached in Karpov – Csom, Bad Lauterberg 1977. Black is a piece up, but White has a strong attack. Find the best move.

Discussion

It's not hard to see that Black has only two viable moves here: 49...♘g5 and 49...♘f8. Black was not in time pressure, so he had time to evaluate both moves. They appear to be comparable since they both save the h7-knight and also guard that square after the knight moves. Most of us will be attracted to 49...♘f8 because it attacks White's rook. If that rook has to move, we gain time to activate our queen with moves such as 50...♛c8 or 50...♛f3.

However, 49...♘f8 loses to the spectacular 50.♘f5!!. Now visualize why White's attack is unstoppable. The problem with 49...♘f8 is that both the h- and g-files are ripped open after 50.♘f5 exf5. Had the knight moved instead to g5, it would have blocked any attacks on the g-file. The lesson here is that anytime we're under attack and the opponent's queen and/ or rook are extremely active, there is a good possibility that he has both direct threats and hidden "geometrical" threats based on the mobility of that major piece. The move 50.♘f5 opens the backward diagonal for the white queen to jump to h2 with a devastating check.

Successfully defending here does not require a lot of calculation. If we consider (before it's too late) the possibility of White's playing 50.♘f5, it's not hard to calculate the variations to confirm that White is winning. In these situations, we need to activate our sense of danger to enable us to "see" these hidden threats. So unless you're short on time, you must consider *every* aggressive response by your opponent before making a move when you're defending and the opponent has mobile major pieces.

T70 (Supplemental Position)

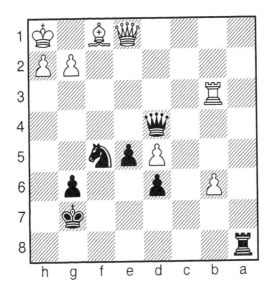

Discussion

Ironically, that same year Karpov (the reigning world champion at the time) fell victim to a similar "backward" geometrical attack against GM Mark Taimanov at Leningrad. In this position, Karpov has just played 37.b6. That loses to the spectacular 37...罝a1 38.罝b1 ♘xg3+ 39.hxg3 罝a8!, and White will be mated!

(This page intentionally left blank)

T71: Black to Move

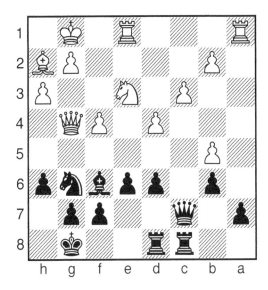

At a 2015 event in New Jersey, I had Black in this position against Boris Privman, a 2350-rated player for most of his adult life. Find three candidate moves and select the best one.

Discussion

Only one move maintains equality for Black: 24...♘e7. Why are all other moves worse? The answer is that White gains a large advantage with the pawn break 25.f5, opening lines for his pieces and giving his opponent an isolated d-pawn (or hanging pawns on e6 and d6). After Black moves the knight to e7, White gains nothing from 25.f5 e5!, when the e7-knight prevents White from playing 26.♘d5. Instead, though, I played the poor move 24...♕d7. There followed 25.f5 ♘f8 26.fxe6 fxe6, and White had a big edge due to Black's hanging pawns. White went on to win.

This position should not be difficult to solve. It's obvious that White plans to play f4-f5. So a simple question for Black is: since I can't stop White from making that move, how can I minimize its impact? Asking that question leads to an obvious answer: 24...♘e7. Instead, I played the "active" 24...♕d7 with the idea of attacking his b-pawn. However, after 25.f5 exf5 26.♘xf5, I can't capture the b-pawn because White then wins the exchange with 27.♘xd6.

These simple variations are not difficult to calculate. When our opponent has the initiative and is planning an unstoppable pawn break, our first priority is to determine the potential impact of that break and find ways to minimize it. Only then should we consider more active moves. My queen move was flawed for an additional reason: If I capture that pawn on b5, White's rook captures my a7-pawn, increasing his initiative to decisive proportions. Holding equal positions that are easier to play for the opponent requires a sense of danger and a "prevention" mentality. This is not rocket science. Rather, it's a mindset that can be developed through training positions like this one.

T72: White to Move

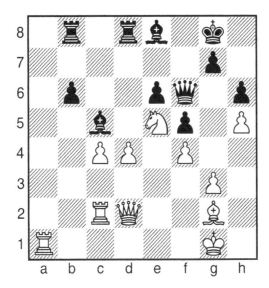

I was Black in this game against expert Michael Hehir (rated 2135) in a 2010 event at the Marshall Chess Club. My last move was 26...♝c5. What should White play in this position?

Discussion

It looks like White is in trouble. If you didn't consider either 27.dxc5 or 27.♗d5, then you chose a losing move! So here's a second chance: Evaluate these two moves and pick the best one.

At first glance, 27.♗d5 seems to save White. However, after 27...exd5 28.dxc5 dxc4 29.♕c3 b5, Black's connected passed pawns give him a winning edge. So the only chance for White is to play the *Transformative* sacrifice 27.dxc5 ♖xd2 28.♖xd2 bxc5 29.♗f3, when the position is equal. White found this sacrifice and the game ended in a draw several moves later.

This is an important training opportunity: Carefully examine the position and explain why it's equal. Where is White's compensation for sacrificing his queen? It consists of the following factors:

- The pawn structure is symmetrical, making it almost impossible for Black to obtain a passed pawn;
- Black doesn't have any pawn breaks to open up the position;
- The e5-knight is a centralized monster that can never be removed;
- The white rooks can easily coordinate to defend any weak points in White's position.

Carefully look at the position one more time while keeping these four factors in mind. This will help you lock this image into your long-term memory so it will be available to you when you face a similar situation in your own games. This type of transformative sacrifice is hard to see. Even when we see it, we often lack the courage to play it. However, when all other moves look bad, we have to take a close look at these types of sacrifices to see if there is dynamic compensation. Often, they are the "only move" to keep you in the game.

T73: Black to Move

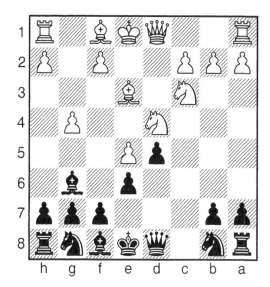

At a 2015 FIDE-rated event at the Marshall Chess Club, I played Black here against NM Rich Shtivelband. Consider the following three candidate moves and select the best one: 8...♞c6, 8...h5, and 8...♛d7. Also, which one is the *worst* choice? That last question is an important part of the exercise, so don't skip it!

Discussion

8...♘c6 gives Black a small advantage and 8...♕d7 is equal. That leaves 8...h5 as the worst choice. Why is it a poor move? Try to answer that before reading my commentary below.

I knew that White was planning a pawn storm with f2-f4-f5. So I decided to immediately attack the g4-pawn with 8...h5, forcing it to either trade on h5 or move forward to g5. Then White's f-pawn lacks the pawn support needed to advance to f5. However, this "plan" was careless, since White simply ignored the attack on his g-pawn and played 9.f4!. White doesn't need the g-pawn to achieve a strong break on f5. After 9...hxg4, White could have entered the line 10.♗b5+ ♘d7 11.f5 ♗xf5 12.♘xf5 exf5 13.♕xd5 when, after castling long, he would have won the d7-knight! Instead, he played the inferior 10.f5 ♗xf5 11.♘xf5 exf5 12.♕xd5 ♘c6 and I was better!

Going back to the starting position, it's clear that White is way ahead in development and has a clear plan (the pawn storm f2-f4-f5). Also, he can castle long in just two moves while Black is many moves away from getting his king to a safe place. Also, except for the bishop on g6, all of Black's pieces are on their original squares. Those factors should have been a warning sign that a *Counter-Attacking* move like ...h7-h5 was doomed to fail since there's nothing to back up that lonely pawn's "attack." That pawn was like a poodle trying to take down a pit bull by biting its ankle!

T74: Black to Move

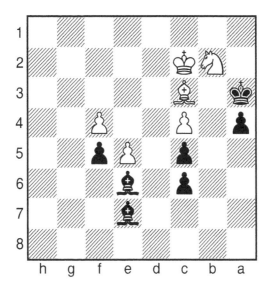

This position is from Anand – Topalov, Melody Amber 2005. Black has an extra pawn but his king stands in its way. What is Black's best move?

Discussion

I'm sure that many readers chose 45...♗f8. This is a waiting move that appears to tie the white knight down to b2 since it needs to defend the c4-pawn. That's the move that Topalov chose too. It loses by force: White now plays 46.♘d3 and Black can't prevent mate in two (47.♗b2 followed by 48.♘c1#).

If you sensed that this is an *Only Move* situation, you were correct. All moves lose except for one. Now go back to the diagram and see if you can find it (if you're not sure what it is). Remember, the technique for solving "only move" positions is that you must consider *every* reasonable move. Ironically, the first time you encountered that advice in this book was in Position T6, where Topalov (yes, the same guy) resigned against Carlsen instead of finding the drawing move. Topalov has always been a fierce attacker but is far less skilled as a defender.

The saving move is 45...♚a2!. Without moving the pieces on your board or in your chess app, visualize why that move enables Black to draw. Don't skip this exercise.

T75: White to Move

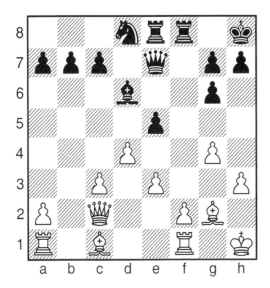

At the 2011 U.S. Amateur Team Championship, I was White in this position against NM Ilya Krasik. The position is equal. Find three candidate moves and select the best one.

Discussion

Stockfish indicates that these are the four best candidates: 19.f3, 19.f4, 19.♖b1, and 19.dxe5. The first three give Black a small plus. The last one results in a fully equal position. I played a much inferior move, 19.♗d2. Then after 19...e4! establishing a spearhead pawn on my half of the board, Black has a large advantage. Note how his bishop is aiming for my king while my c1-bishop is shut out of play. It didn't take long for Black to build a winning attack: 20.c4 c6 21.c5 ♗b8 22.f4 exf3 23.♖xf3 ♖xf3 24.♗xf3 ♕h4 25.♗g2 ♕g3 26.♔g1 ♖f8 and mate on h2 is unstoppable.

Now let's go back to the diagram. Evaluate why 19.e4 is not a good move (it's the worst of the four alternatives that *Stockfish* identified). It appears to grab space in the center, but Black has fully developed pieces while White's queenside pieces have not moved yet. That should be a warning sign that White is not prepared to advance the center pawns since he's not ready to fully protect them and they could become juicy targets for Black's pieces. For example, after 19...♘e6, Black's knight is threatening to jump into f4 while also threatening my d4-pawn after first exchanging pawns on d4 (...exd4).

I rejected the best move (19.dxe5) purely on positional grounds: I didn't want to create an isolated c-pawn and also saw that after 19...♕xe5, the only way to stop checkmate is to play 20.f4, leaving my e3-pawn backward on an open file! Thus it appeared that 19.dxe5 would leave me with *two* bad pawns. However, after this trade, Black no longer has any center pawns and his bishop is restrained following 20.f4. The e3-pawn is easily defended with ♗d2 and ♖ae1. Then White may soon have an opportunity to advance the pawn to e4 with a serious space advantage. Also, that e4-pawn could turn into a monster passed pawn in an endgame. That's why this variation leads to a dynamically equal position with chances for both sides.

This position was another case of reacting to a "phantom" threat. When we're considering a move like 19.dxe5 but then see the black queen sitting on e5 threatening mate in one, our brain triggers what's called an "amygdala hijack." In this position, my brain was screaming, *"don't play that move!"* When the hijack is triggered, we immediately abandon that idea and look for a "safer" one, instead of calmly evaluating whether the threat is real or not. You can prevent or stop an amygdala hijack by breathing deeply, slowing down, and trying to focus your thoughts. This allows your frontal cortex (the part that is responsible for logical, analytical thinking) to regain control.

This training position covered several important topics: failure to see the threat posed by Black's 19...e4 *(Prevention)*, avoiding grabbing space (e.g., 19.e4) before we're fully developed *(Activity)*, and the role of strong emotions in causing us to abandon potentially promising moves too quickly before the logical part of the brain has an opportunity to evaluate them.

(This page intentionally left blank)

T76: Black to Move

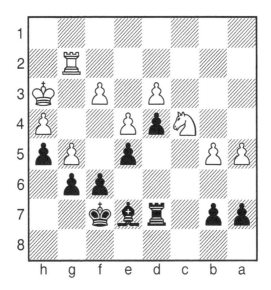

I had Black here against NM Yevgeny Feldman in a 2013 Swiss at the Marshall Chess Club. White is slightly better due to his more active rook and good knight vs. bad bishop. However, Black has excellent drawing chances. Find three candidate moves and decide on the best one.

Discussion

Most of the P-R-O-A-C-T defensive methods don't seem to apply in this position, except for "A" *(Activity)*. When we're forced to defend passively with no opportunity to implement an active *plan,* we still need to ensure that we have active *pieces.* In such cases, we must look for moves that optimize the mobility and flexibility of our pieces and make sure that they are coordinating well. Just using that principle should be enough to suggest that 41...♖d8 is a logical candidate move.

A simple count will show that from d7, the rook can only move to two safe squares (d8 and c7). When on d8, that rook can now go to eight safe squares. Do the math: Eight versus two is a difference of 400%! I played 41...♗d8. That poor move boxes in my rook and also puts the bishop on a passive square. Watch how easy it was for Black to drift into a losing position: 42.a6 bxa6 43.bxa6 ♖c7 44.♖b2 and White seized the open file with a winning advantage. That approach doesn't work for White if Black plays the active 41...♖d8. Then 42.a6 bxa6 43.bxa6 ♖b8!, and Black is the one who takes the open file!

This example provides a graphic example of how easy it is to drift into a losing position by not giving attention to the flexibility and mobility of our pieces. Of the P-R-O-A-C-T defensive methods, "A" *(Activity)* is the most universal since we must always be on the lookout for candidate moves that provide activity, even when the overall strategy in these passive positions is to "hold the fort." In other words, even when there is no active plan available to us, active pieces are essential to maximize our chances of drawing the game.

T77: Black to Move

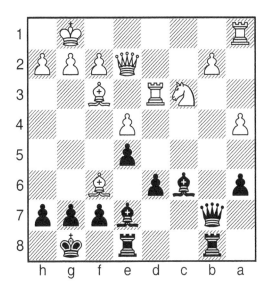

In 2002 at a Marshall Chess Club event, I held the black pieces in this position against Fabiano Caruana. At the time of this game, he was nine years old and had a FIDE rating of 2032. Everyone knows that he is now the #2 player in the world. Fabiano has just played 24.♗xf6. How would you recapture his bishop? To get full credit, you need to be able to explain why your choice is better than the alternative.

Discussion

At first glance, each move has its pluses and minuses. 24...♗xf6 would maintain a healthy pawn structure in front of my king but allow White to capture my d6-pawn. The alternative recapture 24...gxf6 damages my pawn structure but allows me to defend my d6-pawn. Then after 25...♔h8 and 26...♖g8, my rook can attack down the g-file and also helps defend my king (e.g., it can move to g7). After considering these pros and cons, I decided to play 24...gxf6.

Is my commentary above similar to your own evaluation of the position? If so, did you choose the same move as me? If you did, your evaluation was as superficial as mine was during the game! That move gives White a decisive advantage. In contrast, after 24...♗xf6 25.♖xd6 ♗e7 26.♖d2 a5, the position is completely equal. To gain the greatest value from this exercise, explain how Black is fully equal even though he's a pawn down with a backward d-pawn on an open file.

Black is equal because:

- He has the bishop pair in an open position;
- His major pieces on the b-file exert huge pressure on the b2-pawn (it's backward and on an open file) and down the entire b-file; White will find it almost impossible to mobilize this extra pawn;
- Black's dark-squared bishop will be a monster piece after transferring to the d4 square via c5.

As discussed in T75, this is another case of "amygdala hijacking," where the fear of giving up a central pawn was so strong that my brain refused to consider 24...♗xf6. In cases where we realize that *not* giving up a pawn could be extremely dangerous (as it was here because it ruined my king's fortress), we must calmly visualize what moves are likely to be made after our opponent wins that pawn and then determine if there is genuine compensation. Had I applied that level-headed approach during the game, I would have "seen" these compensating factors as summarized above.

Since Caruana is now a chess "rock star," you may be curious how the game turned out. After my mistake, Fabiano misplayed the attack and slowly drifted into a losing position. I went on to win a memorable game:

24...gxf6 25.♖b1 a5 26.♗h5 ♗f8 27.♕g4+ ♔h8 28.♕h4 ♗g7 29.♖h3 h6 30.♔h1 f5 31.f3 fxe4 32.fxe4 ♖f8 33.♗f3 f5 34.♕e1 fxe4 35.♗xe4 d5 36.♗c2 ♖f7 37.♕g3 ♖bf8 38.♗d3 e4 39.♗e2 d4 40.♘b5 ♗xb5 41.axb5 d3 42.♗xd3 exd3 43.♕xd3 ♕e4 44.♖g1 ♕xd3 45.♖xd3 ♗xb2 46.h4 a4 47.g4 a3 48.♖b3 ♖f1 **0-1**

T78: White to Move

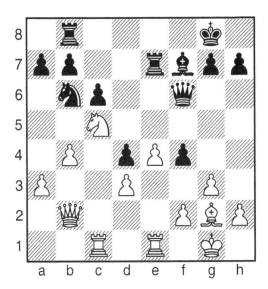

At a 2021 event at the Atlanta Chess Center, I was White here against Ethan Sheehan (USCF 2180). Black has just played 25...f4. Find three candidate moves for White and choose the best one.

Discussion

White is slightly better here due to his strong knight (e.g., it puts pressure on the b7-pawn) and Black's weak pawn on d4. I did not see a way for Black to build a serious attack on my king, so I snatched the pawn with 26.gxf4 ♛xf4 27.♛xd4. Believe it or not, 26.gxf4 was not even among *Stockfish's* top 10 moves! Many other moves are better than 26.gxf4 (e.g., 26.♛d2, 26.♔h1, 26.♘h3, 26.a4, 26.♗f1, 26.h4, and 26.♛e2). It's not a blunder, but it allows Black to equalize. Evaluate why winning a pawn in this position was not a good decision.

Two reasons:

- White damages the structure in front of his king, which will give Black attacking chances sooner or later. This was the same problem with my decision to play 24...gxf6 in my game against Caruana;

- Since I now have to guard my king, it will be a long time before I can utilize that extra pawn. In the meantime, Black's position will be easier to play. That means that White's chances of making a mistake are higher than Black's (see the next position).

T79: White to Move

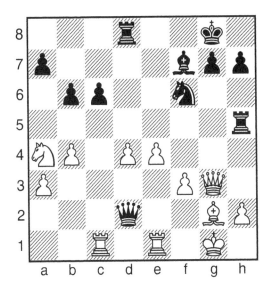

This is later in my game against Ethan Sheehan. Recall what I said in the last position regarding the potential danger in a position that is objectively equal (according to a strong chess engine), but is easier for our opponent to play. In such situations the likelihood of our making a significant mistake is a lot higher than that of our opponent's making one (assuming the opponents are fairly close in playing strength). This position is a perfect example. It is fully equal but easier for Black to play. Find three candidates moves for White and choose the best one.

Discussion

I thought I had a significant advantage thanks to my extra pawn and total control of the center with my pawns on d4 and e4. His attack seemed easy to defend against. That d4-pawn is the crown jewel in my position, so my only thought was that I needed to defend it. Therefore, I played 34.♖ed1 after contemplating the position for only 30 seconds.

As noted in the Introduction, it's dangerous when defending (or when the position is tricky) to treat the position like it's a fill-in-the-blank test by only considering one move. It's crucial in these cases to increase our odds of finding the "answer" by converting the situation into a multiple-choice test via the identification of candidate moves. You probably know where I'm going with this: My move was a major mistake. After 34...♕e3+ 35.♕f2 (if 35.♔h1, then 35...♘xe4 is crushing) 35...♕xf2+ 36.♔xf2 ♗b3, Black is winning.

White's two best moves involve the defensive methods of *Activity* and *Transformation:* One approach is to "let" Black capture that crown-jewel pawn on d4 with 34.♘c3 ♕xd4+ 35.♔h1 ♖e8 36.f4 and White has a small advantage, while the other is to actively sacrifice it with 34.d5 cxd5 35.e5 and White is slightly better. He has a monster passed pawn on e5 and an open c-file for his rook, while Black's d5-pawn is isolated and his knight must now move to a passive square (d7 or e8). Now it's White's game that's easier to play!

I've said it numerous times: Highly passive moves can be deadly. This position takes that one step further by showing how a *greedy* passive move (holding on to that d4-pawn at all costs) can be worse. This example shows why we must quickly scan the board for the full range of P-R-O-A-C-T defensive candidate moves when the position is tricky and our opponent is more active. The two pawn sacrifices above buy time for White to neutralize Black's activity and coordinate his pieces.

T80: Black to Move

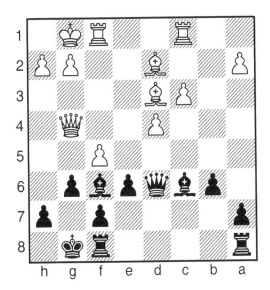

Here I was Black here against a player rated 1960 in a 2013 FIDE-rated event at the Marshall Chess Club. Come up with three candidate moves and choose the best one for Black.

Discussion

White has just played 18.f5, sacrificing a pawn to open lines for his active pieces. That move heightened my emotional state. One reaction ("fight") is to respond immediately and capture that intruder with 18... exf5 (the chess version of *"there's no point in thinking about it, so I'll just swat that bug off my arm"*). At the other extreme (flight), an emotional reaction would be to only consider highly cautious moves like 18...♔h8.

Instead of these emotion-based decisions, there is a better solution that emerges when we calmly look for multiple candidate moves: 18... h5! *(Counter-Attack)*. This gave me a large advantage after 19.♕h3 exf5, when I'm up a pawn and have strengthened the pawn fortress around my king. Observant readers will remember that this is the same position that appeared in the Introduction to illustrate the fight-or-flight response that is triggered when we're facing danger.

The lesson here is that when we are faced with danger on the chessboard, it's easy to overlook simple counter-attacking moves like 18...h5. The emotional centers in our brain that are highly attuned to danger reject these moves even before we're consciously aware of it. The only solution is to sit on your hands, breathe deeply, calm down, and force yourself to find at least three candidate moves. If you take those steps, counter-attacking moves like 18...h5 are not hard to see.

T81: Black to Move

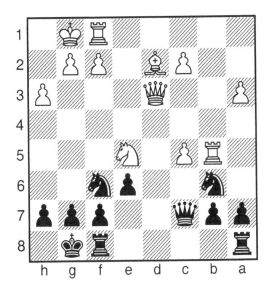

In a 2020 event at the Atlanta Chess Center, I had Black here. Find three candidate moves and choose the best one.

Discussion

My knight is under attack, so the obvious choices are 1...♘bd5 and 1...♘bd7. Both of these keep the black knight centralized. They are the first moves that capture our attention. With two choices to work with, the brain wants to "get on with it" by then figuring out which one is better. The first one gives White a solid edge because the d5-knight will soon be kicked away when White plays c2-c4. Then White will play ♗d2-f4 and the position is very dangerous for Black.

The second one leads to a roughly equal position but is slightly easier for White to play (e.g., 1...♘bd7 2.♘xd7 ♘xd7 3.♕f3.) However, 1...♘a4! is more active than those two choices and gives Black a small advantage since it attacks White's c5-pawn while keeping the other knight near the king to provide defensive support. I played the inferior 1...♘bd5 and two moves later we reached the next position.

T82: Black to Move

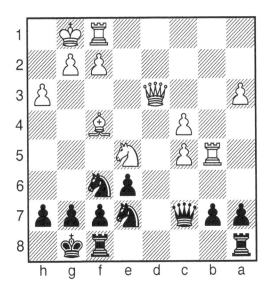

Find three candidate moves and choose the best one. Most players as Black in this position would be feeling the danger. In the military, the highest level of danger is referred to as DEFCON 1. For individual human beings, it's called "fight or flight."

Discussion

Only one move gives Black rough equality and it's far from an obvious one: 1...♘f5. The alternative 1...♘c6 gives White an edge but Black is still fighting. All other moves give White a decisive advantage! Hence the solution involves a combination of *Activity* and *Counter-Attack*. After 1...♘f5, White has no way to exploit the vulnerable position of the black queen vis-à-vis White's f4-bishop (e.g., 1...♘f5 2.♖fb1 ♖ad8 3.♖xb7 ♕xe5!).

I played the poor "flight" move 1...♕c8 and, after 2.♖fb1, quickly fell into a lost position. The lesson here is that effective defensive play requires tactical alertness and concrete calculation. It's impossible to play good defense simply by avoiding blunders and playing cautious moves. The *Activity, Counter-Play,* and *Transformative* defensive methods (A-C-T) demand a high degree of tactical alertness and a willingness to engage in the hard work of calculating variations. The move 1...♕c8 is what we may call a "positional blunder," meaning that it is the equivalent of hanging material in terms of the negative impact on our position.

T83: Black to Move

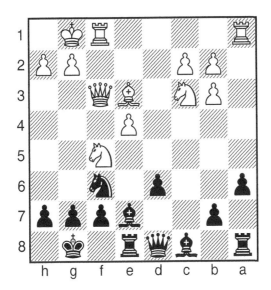

I handled Black here against NM James West at a 2011 event at the Marshall Chess Club. Find three candidate moves and choose the best one.

Discussion

While quickly scanning for candidate moves, I identified three possibilities based on the preliminary reasoning in parentheses:

- 14...♗f8 (this saves my bishop pair, defends g7, and opens the file for my rook to pressure Black's e4-pawn);
- 14...♗e6 (this completes my development and connects my major pieces on the first rank);
- 14...♗xf5 (this removes the dangerous knight but gives up the bishop pair; now White's next four moves are likely to be ♕xf5-♗g5-♗xf6-♘d5 with a monster knight on d5).

Which of these possibilities would you choose? Only the last one yields full equality. The first one gives White a winning position and the second one gives White a significant advantage. Now that you have the "answer key," take a few minutes to determine why 14...♗f8 is losing (hint: start with the simple 15.♘h6+). The refutation of 14...♗e6 is not as obvious, but still fairly straightforward: 15.♘xg7 ♔xg7 16.♗d4 and White is much better.

We should not be too hard on ourselves if our preliminary reasons for candidate moves later prove to be flawed. That's why they're called "preliminary" (i.e., they occur during the initial identification of candidate moves). Preliminary reasons are just a starting point for a deeper evaluation of the candidate moves. If we rely on our initial reasons as a basis for making a move, often they will prove to be superficial and flawed. For example, notice how the so-called advantages I listed above for 14...♗f8 seem reasonable on the surface, but have a simple refutation.

The next step after coming up with good reasons for a move is to verify that the move works from a tactical standpoint. Verbal evaluations should never substitute for verification through the calculation of short variations. This verification rarely needs to go beyond 2-3 moves. Perhaps the best example in this book of relying on superficial verbal evaluation instead of verification, resulting in a losing move, was Position T1. At the critical moment, I told myself that I couldn't play 15...♗e7. In fact, that would have been the winning move!

T84: Black to Move

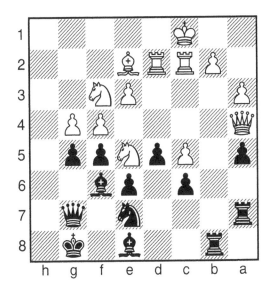

I was Black here against the late NM Jerry Simon in a 2005 event at the Marshall Chess Club. The position is complicated due to the pawn tension on the kingside. Positions with pawn tension require extra vigilance, especially for the defender, because one or more exchanges can quickly change the dynamics of the position. Find three candidate moves for Black and select the best one.

Discussion

It's hard to believe, but only one move gives Black an edge. All others give White an advantage ranging from small to winning! Now that you know this, have you changed your mind on the move you chose? OK, before I comment on the best move, gain some additional practice by evaluating these three candidate moves: 35...fxg4, 35...gxf4, and 35...♖ab7.

In the game, I played 35...fxg4. There followed 36.♘xg4 ♗g6 37.♘xf6+ ♕xf6 38.♗d3 ♗xd3 39.♖xd3 gxf4 40.exf4. Look closely at this position and explain why White stands better. This is a crucial visualization exercise. Successful defense requires accurate evaluation of the final position after a series of moves. The primary reasons for White's advantage here are his superior pawn structure and his more-active pieces. I have weak pawns on a5 and c6 that require constant protection by my pieces.

The move 35...gxf4 would be great for Black if White recaptured with 36.exf4. However, 36.♕xf4! is much stronger and gives White a big plus because, for starters, his queen has tactical threats on the unprotected b8-rook. But more importantly, after White plays ♗e2-d3, his rooks will swing over to the kingside and Black's king and queen will be in hot water, with the rooks too far away to help! This is another one of those lightning attacks that appear to come out of nowhere! Improper release of pawn tension can serve as a "trigger" for this type of rapid assault since files and diagonals come open very quickly after one or two exchanges of those pawns.

The move 35...♖ab7 gives Black an advantage. A training opportunity: Take some time to determine why that's the case, based on the insights you gained from reading the commentary above about the two inferior choices 35...fxg4 and 35...gxf4. The main reason is that the rook is now much more active. For example, White can't snatch a pawn with 36.♕xa5 because then 36...gxf4 gives Black a huge advantage as White can no longer recapture with 37.♕xf4.

More often than not when there is pawn tension, the first player to release the tension by initiating a pawn trade hands the initiative over to the opponent, especially if the opponent can recapture that pawn with a piece that places it on a more active square than before (35...gxf4 above allowed White's queen to quickly transfer to the kingside where it could combine with the rooks to start a dangerous attack on the black king).

When we're defending and there is pawn tension in the position, this usually leads to emotional tension. The impulse in these situations is to relieve this uncomfortable feeling (a form of "flight") as soon as possible by making one or more pawn exchanges. In many cases, that backfires because the opponent's recaptures increase the activity of his pieces.

The lesson here is: When you're defending and there is pawn tension, sit on your hands and identify at least two candidate moves that *don't* release that tension. There will be cases where the best move is to release the tension, but many more cases where this is a poor approach. By calmly finding those additional candidate moves, your odds of mounting a successful defense go up considerably.

(This page intentionally left blank)

T85: Black to Move

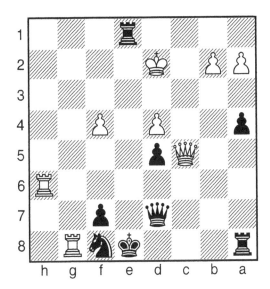

Hochstrasser – Ziatdinov, Bern Open 1994. In this position, Black is a piece up but his e1-rook is under attack and White threatens mate on f8. If Black defends against that threat, White can strengthen the mating attack by playing ≅hh8. Find three candidate moves for the second player and choose the best one.

Discussion

It probably didn't take you long to realize that Black is in trouble and that White's threats seem unstoppable. So instead of resigning prematurely like Topalov did against Carlsen (T6), your task is to find the "only move" to save Black. As you'll recall from previous *Only Move* training positions in this book, that means you must quickly identify *every* reasonable candidate move, instead of diving deep into the first move that captures your attention. Most of us can remember times when we went down that rabbit hole and spent a long time (more than 10 minutes) focusing on just one move and then rejected it. So instead of chasing the first rabbit that caught your attention here, jot down all of those candidate moves before reading the commentary below.

Here are the main ones: 1...♕e7, 1...♔d8, 1...♖e2+, and 1...♖e7. After identifying every reasonable candidate, you must use the method of "elimination," a technique discussed by GM Jacob Aagaard in his *Grandmaster Preparation* series of tactical training books. To paraphrase Jacob, when there are a number of moves and all appear to be unsatisfactory, it's essential to work backwards by weeding out the losing moves first instead of trying to immediately figure out which one is best. The way to do this for each candidate move is to ask yourself, *"If I play this move, how can my opponent refute it?"* This requires tactical calculation, but usually no more than 2-3 moves deep. Go ahead and try this for each of the four candidate moves, starting with 1...♕e7. Clearly visualize White's likely reply.

With patience, you can find the refutation for each of the first three candidate moves. The last candidate (1...♖e7) saves the e1-rook from capture by the white king and also stops the mate threat on f8. Not hard to see that this is "working" so far, right? Now if White renews the mating threat with 2.♖hh8, find the best move for Black. This is a moment where visualization is more important than calculation. In fact, no calculation at all is required to find the saving move: 2...♕e6!. This gives the king an escape square on d7, protects against a check by the white queen on c6, and threatens a counter-attack with 3...♕e2+. Black is fully equal and White needs to be careful (e.g., 3.♖xf8+ ♔d7 4.♖xa8 ♕e1+ 5.♔d3 ♖e3+ 6.♔c2 ♖e2+ 7.♔d3 ♕d2#). A successful evacuation from mortal danger worthy of the great escape artist Harry Houdini!

In summary, the thinking method for solving "only-move" positions consists of three elements:

- Find *every* reasonable candidate move;
- Use the method of elimination to weed out the bad ones;
- Use "15-second Freeze Frame" visualization to fully "see" the position (refer to Positions T11, T36, T41, and T54 for prior examples of this Freeze Frame technique).

T86: Black to Move

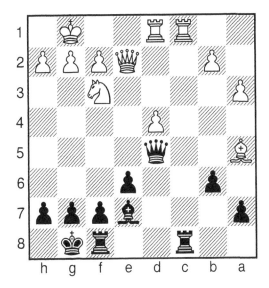

I was Black here against a 1940-rated player in a 2017 event at the Marshall Chess Club. White has just captured my knight (1.♗xa5). There are only three reasonable candidate moves: 1...♖xc1, 1...♕xa5, and 1...bxa5. Evaluate them and choose the best one.

Discussion

One of the most important defensive skills is accuracy in situations where we have multiple ways to recapture a pawn or a piece. Our preliminary evaluation of these moves might include the following observations:

- If I play 1...bxa5, I damage my queenside pawn structure and White can play 2.♕a6 to attack those weak pawns;
- If I play 1...♕xa5, I release the blockade on White's isolated d-pawn, allowing him to eliminate it with 3.d5 (after exchanging a pair of rooks on c8). I can't take it with 3...exd5 because White captures my e7-bishop;
- 1...♖xc1 seems fine, but then I still need to decide how to capture the a5-bishop.

Thus it appears that we need to choose between "the lesser of two evils" (1...♕xa5 or 1...bxa5). Which one would you choose and why? In such cases, you must consider some additional factors to help you make the right choice. One factor is whether or not you are in time pressure. The move 1...♕xa5, allowing White to play d4-d5 (after exchanging a pair of rooks on c8), requires some calculation because this push threatens to win the e6-pawn. Evaluating this variation will consume precious time on the clock. The alternative (1...bxa5) keeps the queen on the centralized blockading square, preventing the complications that result from 1...♕xa5. The second factor to consider is whether you are playing for a win or a draw. That will depend on your opponent's rating and other factors (e.g., needing a victory to win a cash prize). Which move do you think is better if you're playing for a win?

If that's your goal, then clearly 1...bxa5 is the better choice. It prevents White from liquidating his isolated d4-pawn and opens the b-file for a black rook to put pressure on White's b2-pawn. Both recaptures give Black an equal position, but *Stockfish* evaluates 1...bxa5 as slightly better for Black.

T87: Black to Move

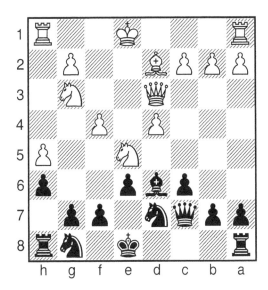

Here I had Black against an expert-level player in a 2017 event at the Marshall Chess Club. Find three candidate moves and pick the best one.

Discussion

An important defensive skill in the opening and early middlegame is the proper sequencing of planned moves. As an example, in this position I could first play 13...♘gf6 (the natural destination for the knight) followed by ...♖ad8 (the natural square for this rook since it will be active on the semi-open d-file). Or I could reverse the order of those two moves. It doesn't appear to make much difference. Which order would you choose and why?

Turns out there is a meaningful difference. After 13...♘gf6 14.0-0-0 ♖d8 15.♘e4, White is slightly for preference. In contrast, after 13...♖d8, Black is threatening to win a pawn by capturing twice on e5. So instead of continuing his development with 14.0-0-0, White must take time to defend against this threat (e.g., by moving his queen to f3 or e2). So 13... ♖d8 gives Black a precious tempo in his efforts to complete his development. These types of rook moves that contain veiled threats are what I call "loading the gun" (see Position T53 for another example). I played 13...♖d8 and went on to win a nice positional game.

The lesson here is that anytime you are faced with a situation where your next few moves are a "given," you must consider whether or not the move order makes a difference. This is especially important when playing Black, where one tempo can spell the difference between equality and an initiative for our opponent.

T88: Black to Move

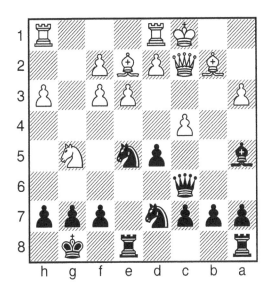

In the 2017 West Orange (NJ) Chess Club Championship, I was Black here against expert Lev Zilbermintz. His last move was 16.♘g5, threatening 17.♕xh7+. Find three candidate moves and choose the best one.

Discussion

The first moves that come to mind are 16...♘f6, 16...♘f8, and 16...g6. All defend the h7-pawn. However, all of them also give White a large advantage! Every one of these candidates is passive. That should be a clue that we should look for one *Active* move to add to our "multiple-choice test." Once we remind ourselves to do that, it's easier to find 16...h6!. Then after 17.♕h7+ ♔f8, White's attack looks dangerous but Black can defend by walking a tightrope: 18.f4 ♘xc4 19.♗xg7+ ♔e7, and Black achieves full dynamic equality in a complicated position because his threat of a discovered check by moving the knight from c4 limits the first player's options and buys time for Black to organize his defense. In fact, after 19...♔e7, White has only *one* move to keep the balance: 20.♘xf7. All other moves give Black a large advantage!

Notice how double-edged the variations are after 16.♘g5. Black now has only one way to maintain the balance (16...h6), while after 19...♔e7, it is White who must find the only way to achieve equality. So this position is all about the active defensive methods of *Activity, Counter-Attack,* and *Transformation* (A-C-T).

T89: Black to Move

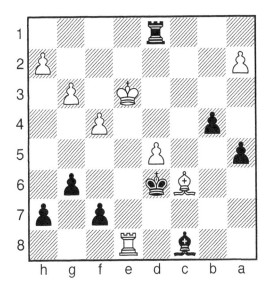

In a FIDE-rated event at the Marshall Chess Club in 2016, I was Black here against NM Ed Frumkin. Find three candidate moves and choose the best one.

Discussion

The rook's attack on my bishop limits my options. One obvious candidate move is 1...♖e1+ to exchange the rooks. It's also obvious that this move gives Black only equality since White's king will be more active than mine after it goes to d4. If I was short of time or moved without thinking, I might have played the "fork" 1...♗d7. But that is refuted by the simple reply 2.♖d8. By always trying to include at least one *Active* move on our lists of candidates, 1...♗f5 becomes an obvious choice: Not only does it protect the bishop, it is ready for a decisive counter-attack on White's a2-pawn starting with ...♗f5-b1.

I chose the lazy 1...♖e1+ and exchanged the rooks. We agreed to a draw a few moves later. Instead, 1...♗f5 gives Black a winning position. The reason for this mental lapse is that I was tired after almost three hours of play and had been in a defensive mental stance for over an hour. So when we arrived at this position, I did not have the energy or the mindset to notice that the position is winning. Therefore, I instinctively played 1...♖e1+ so that I could finally "relax" and never considered moving the bishop. It's not hard to see that after 1...♗f5, White is in big trouble due to his passive bishop and the lonely and indefensible pawn on a2.

Although this is not a defensive training position per se since I have a winning advantage, my oversight was caused in large part by my defensive mindset that was required over the prior hour of play. Especially when our energy is low, it's hard to shift this mental stance to an offensive one. The reverse is even more common. There are many examples where a player had a winning attack but misplayed it, requiring them to shift gears into defensive mode. That is one of the most difficult mental adjustments to make during a chess game when emotions are heightened.

T90: Black to Move

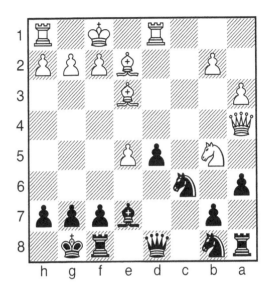

In a 2017 FIDE event at the Marshall Chess Club, I was playing Black here against Szymon Rudowski (rated 2020 at the time of this game). Find three candidate moves and choose the best one.

Discussion

The obvious candidates are 15...♘d7, 15...♘xe5, and 15...axb5.The first one is equal. The second one is slightly better for White after 15...♘xe5 16.♘c3 and White will win the d5-pawn and have the bishop pair in an open position. Then I looked closely at the line 15...axb5 16.♕xa8 ♕c7 17.♖c1 ♘d7 18.♕a7 ♖c8, when White's queen is trapped. However, then I noticed that instead of 17.♖c1, my opponent could play 17.♗xb5 and now White appears to have an escape square on a4 for his queen after I play 17...♘d7. So I rejected 15...axb5 and played 15...♘d7.

Only when replaying the game later did I see that 17.♗xb5 loses for White because my knight plays, *not* 17...♘d7, but 17...♘a6! trapping the queen. This was a case where the first variation I calculated (with my knight going to d7) heavily influenced my perception of the second variation, where the knight needs to go to a *different* square to trap the queen. I made the subconscious assumption that the knight's move to d7 was an essential part of the plan to trap his queen. Therefore, 17...♘a6 was invisible to me during the calculation of the second variation involving 17.♗xb5.

Had I only calculated the second variation and never seen the first one, it would have been easy to find 17...♘a6 since I would have not been operating under the delusion that 17...♘d7 was a required part of the plan. The old cliché says that "seeing is believing." However, there are many cases where it's the reverse: "believing is seeing." Our beliefs determine what we see (17...♘d7 in the first variation) and what remains invisible (17...♘a6 in the second variation).

The only way to overcome this type of chess delusion is to freeze-frame each move when we're calculating a "do-or-die" variation (i.e., one where the outcome will give us a big advantage if we calculate correctly and a big disadvantage if we miscalculate). Sacrificing an exchange with 15...axb5 in an attempt to win White's queen would have been a do-or-die undertaking. Before burning that bridge, you need to remind yourself to slow down during your calculations to freeze-frame the position after *every* move in the sequence.

T91: Black to Move

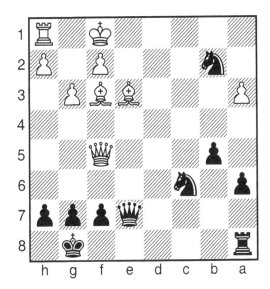

This is later in the same game against Rudowski. He has just played 25.♗f3. Find three candidate moves and choose the best one.

Discussion

I'm a pawn up, but White has significant compensation based on his extremely active bishop pair, my wayward knight on b2, and the attack on my c6-knight. Black has to tread very carefully here. Reasonable candidate moves are 25...g6, 25...♕d6, and 25...♕e8. I played 25...g6, which would have led to equality after 26.♕d5. Instead, White played the seemingly winning 26.♕c2. But I was ready for that! Before reading the commentary that follows, analyze the position after 26.♕c2 to find a way not only to prevent White from winning a piece, but to gain a winning advantage.

After 25...g6 26.♕c2, I played 26...♘c4!. There followed 27.♗xc6 ♖c8 28.♕e4 (apparently saving his bishop, since 28...♕xe4 is met by 29.♗xe4) 28...♘xe3+ 29.fxe3 ♕f6+ and *Black* is the one who wins a piece! As a strong positional player who is less strong in calculating variations, I was proud of this 5-move tactical sequence starting with 25...g6.

The second candidate move (25...♕d6) is poor and gives White a big plus after 26.♗f4. That leaves the third candidate move (25...♕e8). This seemingly passive move is the best choice and gives Black a small advantage. Black has time for such passive play because it will take White two moves to get his rook into the game. Had White's king already been on g2 in the diagram, Black would be lost!

So while 25...g6 was not the strongest of the three candidate moves, it gave me the opportunity to play a memorable 5-move variation that at first appears to lose a piece but actually leads to a winning position!

T92: Black to Move

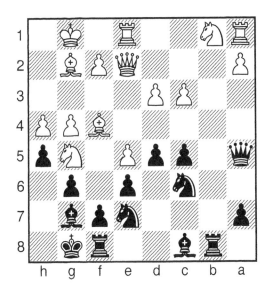

In a 2000 event at the Marshall Chess Club, I was Black here against NM Roman Dubinsky (USCF 2354). He has just played 15.g4, starting an attack on my kingside. Find two candidate moves and choose the best one.

Discussion

When we're playing Black against a much higher-rated opponent, our mindset usually focuses on cautious (P-R-O) methods of defense instead of active (A-C-T) methods, especially in the opening and early middlegame when White usually has a slight lead in development. So that was my mindset after he played g2-g4. I briefly considered 15...hxg4, which will give me the f5 square for my e7-knight. But White's attack looked scary after 16.♕xg4 and 17.h5. However, if I *don't* capture his g-pawn, he will play 16.gxh5 on his next turn with an even scarier attack!

Positions like this are a trigger for heightened emotions, which is the starting point for the "fight-or-flight" reaction we have previously discussed. When our anxiety is heightened and we're feeling threatened, the natural tendency is to fixate on the "danger zone" part of the board (my kingside). This is a form of chess "tunnel vision."

Therefore, although this is not an "only move" situation, you need to treat it like one when the one move that seems necessary to play (15...hxg4 in this example) looks too dangerous. Instead of telling yourself that you "have no choice" but to play that move, you must scan the *whole* board (not just in the "danger zone") for *every* reasonable move. I applied that thought process during the game and spotted the counter-attack 15...♕a4!. Now White is in big trouble due to the hit on the f4-bishop and the g4-pawn. Now that you see it, the move seems obvious. Psychologists call this the "hindsight bias."

However, it's easy to miss a move like this during a tense moment against a much higher-rated player for a few reasons:

- We don't expect a 2350 player to blunder with White on move 15, so we're not "looking" for winning moves. This blindness can even happen to the best players in the world. For example, in Game 6 of the 2014 World Championship match between Carlsen and Anand, they reached this position:

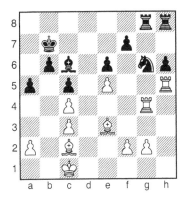

Carlsen played 26.♔d2, an incredible blunder. Anand looked at the position for a few minutes before playing 26...a4. Instead, he could have played the crushing 26...♘xe5 27.♖xg8 ♘xc4+ *(Zwischenzug)* 28.♔d3 ♘b2+ 29.♔d2 ♖xg8 and Black has won two pawns! Anand's blind spot (a form of tunnel vision) was likely caused by subconsciously believing that the best player in the world would not blunder. Of course, the blunder needed to be slightly hidden for Anand to overlook it. Had the position been in a chess puzzle book instead of a game against Carlsen, Anand would have spotted the refutation of 26.♔d2 in about 10 seconds.

- Another reason it would be easy to overlook 15...♕a4 in my game against Dubinsky is that it's a "creeper" move (i.e., one square up the board). The queen is the most powerful piece and it rarely makes a winning move on an open board by moving just one square (unless that move is a check).

- The third reason this move could be missed is that it involves an unusual geometrical pattern where the queen, from the far side of the board, attacks laterally on the opposite side of the board. Our mind is used to thinking of the queen's most powerful moves as vertical (down a file toward our opponent's side of the board) and diagonal. Attacking queen moves across a rank (after first making a creeper move) are rare. Even more difficult to see are "backward" attacking moves by a queen or rook. Perhaps the most famous example in chess history is Karpov–Taimanov (see Supplemental Position T70), where the reigning world champion (playing White) was mated by a brilliant geometrical attack featuring a backward rook move.

(This page intentionally left blank)

T93: White to Move

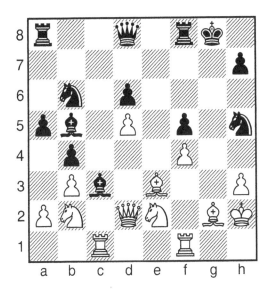

At the 2000 Liberty Bell Open in Philadelphia, I was White here against a 1960-rated player. Black has a space advantage on the queenside and extremely active bishops, and my isolated d5-pawn requires protection. Find three candidate moves and choose the best one.

Discussion

A superficial evaluation of the situation (based on the factors outlined above) would suggest that Black is better. For a couple of minutes after my opponent played his last move (21...♗c3), that's how I felt. So my first instinct was to play the cautious (and passive) 22.♕c2. While that move actually yields an equal position, I rejected it out of fear of 22...♖c8. However, if I had looked a move further instead of emotionally rejecting the queen move as "too dangerous" (that's a feeling, *not* an objective evaluation), I would have noticed that after 22.♕c2 ♖c8 23.♗f3 ♘f6 24.♖g1+, White is on top and Black can't exploit the potential "threat" of a discovered attack on my queen by moving his bishop from c3.

So I started to look for more active moves and noticed the possibility of sacrificing the exchange with 22.♘xc3. If that was not the move you chose, take a moment to calculate the likely next few moves after 22.♘xc3. Then, explain what compensation White gets for his sacrifice before reading my commentary below.

The likely next moves are 22...♗xf1 23.♖xf1 bxc3 24.♕xc3. This is best play and it is also what happened in the game. What is White's compensation in this position? It consists of the following:

- A fabulous bishop pair;
- By using his dark-squared bishop to win the exchange, Black is now fatally weak on the a1-h8 diagonal;
- White has the open g-file to build an attack on Black's exposed king.

The rest of the game is a beautiful illustration of these advantages:

24...♘d7 25.♗f3 ♘hf6 26.♖g1+ ♔f7 27.♖g5 ♖c8 28.♘c4 ♕e7 29.♖xf5 h6 30.♗f2 ♔g7 31.♕xa5 ♖a8 32.♕d2 ♔h8 33.♗d4 ♖g8 34.a4 ♕g7 35.♕f2 ♖a6 36.♕h4 ♔h7 37.♗e4 ♕g6 38.♖xf6 **1-0**

This training position is a nice example of the method of *Transformation* (altering the material balance by a small sacrifice for dynamic compensation). Black's apparent initiative and pressure totally evaporated after I sacrificed the exchange. Not only was it objectively the best move, it forced my opponent to rapidly shift from an attacking mindset to a defensive one. Most players, even world-class ones, have a hard time making that mental and emotional shift. As a result, often their level of play drops significantly.

T94: White to Move

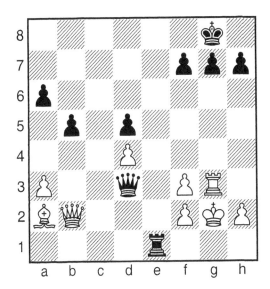

Veltmander – Estrin, Russian Corr. Chp 1960. Identify three candidate moves for White and choose the best one.

Discussion

White is a piece up, but Black has the obvious threat of 1...♕f1#. Most people playing White will likely believe that "I'm winning once I defend against Black's temporary threats." If so, they may reject 1.♔h3 since, after 1...♕f1+ 2.♔g4 ♕d3, there is no way to escape perpetual check on the f-, g-, and h-files, or a threefold repetition of moves starting with 3.♔h3. Because 1.♔h3 is the only king move in the starting position, we turn our attention to rook moves in an attempt to defend and then win the game later with our extra piece. The most reasonable candidate moves are 1.♖g4 and 1.♖g5. Analyze both of those moves by calculating 3-4 moves deep. Hint: Both of them give Black a completely winning attack.

Since the purpose of this book is not to analyze every single candidate move but to provide a training manual for improving your defensive skills and managing your emotions, I won't take up space to document Black's winning moves. Your chess engine will show you the refutations to the two rook moves.

Now let's go back to the starting position and remove the white bishop from the board. You're still facing Black's mate threat, but without that extra piece you no longer have what appears to be a winning position. Therefore your mindset in this case is likely to be "how can I find a way to draw?" instead of "how can I meet his temporary threat and then win with my extra piece?"

I can't prove it, but my hunch is that if you gave the first position to one group of players and the second one to another group of players (let's assume all players in both groups have the same rating), a much higher percentage of players in the second group would find the "only move" (1.♔h3) that allows White to draw.

This is another example of how our mindset can bias our search for candidate moves. If we think we have an advantage when objectively we don't, then the bias will be towards only looking at active "fight" moves (or quickly rejecting "flight" moves like 1.♔h3 that don't allow us to capitalize on our advantage). Sometimes the bias works in reverse, where at first we think our position is worse (e.g., how I felt after my opponent played 21...♗c3 in the previous training position). That mindset caused me (at first) to only consider the passive response 22.♕c2.

The lesson here is that we must put aside emotional "self-talk" about the position (e.g., "I'm winning" or "I'm in trouble") and strive to perform a level-headed analysis of about three candidate moves. For example, after 1.♖g4 in the starting position, calmly visualize Black's potential replies. Hint: Black has three winning moves here, the strongest being 1...h5.

(This page intentionally left blank)

T95: Black to Move

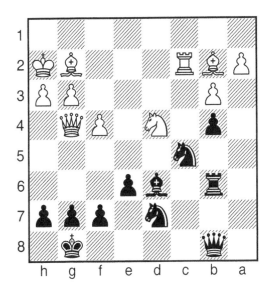

In a 2017 event in New Jersey, I had Black in this position against expert Joshua Hill. Find three candidate moves and select the best one.

Discussion

For starters, Black needs to notice White's veiled threat of mate after the knight moves from d4. This situation, therefore, clearly calls for a cautious *Restraint* type of move. The obvious candidates are 30...g6, 30...♘f6, 30...♗f8, and 30...♕f8. If you picked another move, have your chess engine show you why it's losing. I took less than a minute to choose 30...♘f6. It seemed "totally obvious" based on the following reasoning:

- It places my passive knight on a more active square;
- On f6, the knight helps defend my kingside;
- I gain a tempo by attacking White's queen.

How could any other defensive move in this position top *those* benefits? Well, there is one that could! In reality, the knight move gives White a sizable advantage after 31.♕d1. White has the bishop pair in an open and fluid position. Also, all of White's pieces are coordinating beautifully while Black's pieces are boxed in on the queenside. Notice how the d6-bishop significantly limits the mobility of the black queen and rook. In addition, White has the imminent threat of a knight raid to c6.

The above considerations suggest that 30...♗f8 might be a good defensive move. Based on the above commentary, explain the advantages of this move compared to 30...♘f6. Notice how moving the bishop frees up the d6 "transit square" for use by Black's queen and rook. Now the knight raid (♘d4-c6) can be met with the active and centralizing ...♕b8-d6, instead of the very passive ...♕b8-c7.

The subtle differences between 30...♘f6 and 30...♗f8 provide a vivid example of how easy it is to drift into a losing position without making a blunder or tactical mistake. When we're defending, not only do we need to meet immediate threats, but we must do so in a way that optimizes the activity and coordination of our pieces.

One of the best chess theoreticians in history was Dr. Siegbert Tarrasch. He was among the top three players in the world during the 1890s. He emphasized piece mobility and wrote about the dangers of passive positions. Perhaps his most famous quote is, "Cramped positions contain the germ of defeat."

The most graphic example of this in the entire book is Position T8, where my strong opponent (rated 2440) was playing White. He made no blunders or obvious mistakes during the entire game, yet by playing passively he slowly drifted into a losing position and resigned after only 31 moves. This would be a good time for you to go back and play through that game again. Try to find White's worst move (the one that contributed the most to his loss). It's very hard to find! Don't use your chess engine until you make the effort to find that mysterious move on your own!

(This page intentionally left blank)

T96: Black to Move

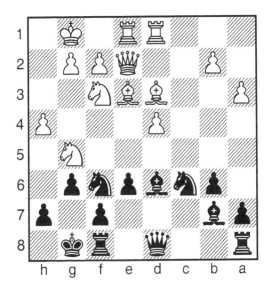

In a 2017 tournament at the West Orange (NJ) Chess Club, I had Black here against NM Vladimir Lipman. Find three candidate moves and choose the best one.

Discussion

White has an active position with offensive potential, while Black has a solid defensive setup and later will be able to attack White's isolated d4-pawn. So the position is dynamically equal. The obvious candidate moves are 1...♕c7, 1...♖c8, 1...♘d5, and 1...♘e7. As in the last training position, there are subtle but important differences between these moves. One example is 1...♖c8 versus 1...♘e7. Explain why the knight move is much better than the rook move.

Notice that the white knights are "redundant" (e.g., the f3-knight can't move to g5 and the g5-knight can't move to f3 – they are getting in each other's way). The knight on g5 is not accomplishing much and would like to reroute to f3 or e4. After 1...♘e7, that g5-knight can't move to e4 because Black's b7-bishop now covers that square. Also, 1...♘e7 repositions this knight on the central d5 square while keeping the other knight on f6 for defensive purposes (e.g., stopping White from playing h4-h5). In contrast, the alternative 1...♖c8 seems active, but allows the g5-knight back into the game by moving to e4. The move 1...♕c7 is less effective than 1...♘e7 for similar reasons. Also, it puts the queen on an open file where it could be inconvenienced by the move of a white rook to c1.

If you think I'm splitting hairs by pointing out minor differences between the candidate moves, bear in mind that awareness of such subtle differences is the most important factor in avoiding the slow drift into a losing position, especially when facing a higher-rated opponent. Providing practice in spotting these subtleties is a major objective of this book.

T97: Black to Move

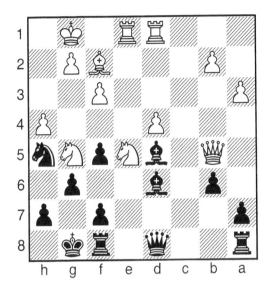

This is a few moves later in my game against Lipman. Find three candidate moves and choose the best one.

Discussion

White threatens to capture my bishop with 23.♕xd5. The obvious candidates are 22...♘f6, 22...♗c7, and 22...♗e7. All of them are solid choices and yield Black a small advantage. So they are safe and would be great choices if you were short on time or energy. However, there is another move that gives Black a larger advantage, but requires some calculation. That move is 22...♘f4. At first it appears to lose a piece since White can play 23.♗e3 (or 23.g3), attacking the knight that is guarding my d5-bishop. But after 23.♗e3, Black plays the *Zwischenzug* 23...a6!, attacking White's queen.

Now after 24.♕d7 ♘h5 25.♕xd8 ♖axd8, Black has a big plus. He has a centralized bishop pair and can tie White down to the defense of his isolated d4-pawn. With the queen trade, White's attacking chances are gone. Also, 22...♘f4 threatens ...h7-h6. Then if the knight moves to h3, the exchange of knights on that square will give White doubled h-pawns and another isolated pawn on f3!

The point of these subtlety exercises where there are several acceptable candidate moves is that they force you to stretch your imagination and visualization skills. That's because there will be many cases where the most complicated choice will be the "only move" path to equality. Honing your mental "radar" to be on the lookout for these seemingly risky methods of defense is essential for players who aspire to increase their playing strength significantly.

T98: Black to Move

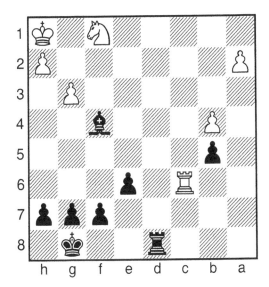

Twice in 2017 I faced prodigy Abhimanyu Mishra in New Jersey events (see T26 for a position from my first game against him). You may recall that he became the youngest IM in history in 2019, just two years after my encounters with him. Here I had Black again. Find three candidate moves and choose the best one.

Discussion

I have a huge advantage here. The top candidate moves are 29...♗g5, 29...♗e5, and 29...♗d6. At first glance, 29...♗g5 seems for choice since it keeps the knight bottled up on f1. However, that's lazy "one-move thinking" since then White can respond with 30.♖b6 and win my b5-pawn (30...♖d5 allows 31.♖b8+, forcing me to play the awkward 31...♗d8). After the second candidate move (29...♗e5), White plays 30.♖c5. Best play is then 30...f6 31.♖xb5 ♖d1 32.♔g2 ♗d4 33.a4 ♖a1 and Black has a large advantage.

The best move is 29...♗d6. It immediately attacks the b4-pawn, forcing White to protect it with 30.a3. Then Black plays 30...♗f8! preventing back-rank mating threats by the white rook, thus freeing up my own rook for active operations. Now White is forced into defensive mode with 31.♖a6 to prevent 31...♖a8, or 31.♖c3 to guard the a3-pawn from the side. It's amazing how a seemingly mild move like 30...♗f8 can force your opponent onto the defense! The reason is that it fully activates the black rook (there is no longer a back-rank mate threat) while driving the white rook into total passivity. So it's really an active move disguised as a passive one. I played the inferior 29...♗g5 (based on the superficial "one-move thinking" mentioned above) and eventually lost the game.

T99: Black to Move

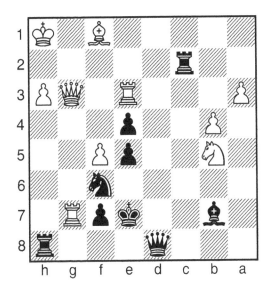

At Lone Pine 1976, the young IM Kim Commons was White against the legendary GM Miguel Najdorf. Find three candidate moves for Black and identify the best one.

Discussion

The first instinct is to protect against ♕xe5+ by playing 37...♕d5. Another good move is 37...♖d2. Then the likely continuation is 38.♕xe5+ ♔f8 39.♖g2 ♖d5. Both of these candidate moves give Black a fully equal game. However, 37...♔f8! is completely winning for Black! By evacuating the king, the capture 38.♕xe5 would no longer come with check and it would allow Black to take the now-loose rook with 38...♔xg7. So the king move combines attack (on the g7-rook) and defense (against the check).

After 37...♔f8 38.♖g5 ♖c1, White is almost in *Zugzwang*. A move by the e3-rook would allow Black to play ...e4-e3 with a discovered check by the b7-bishop. The queen can't protect the f1-bishop with 39.♕g1 since 39...♘h5 leads to unstoppable threats.

T100: Black to Move

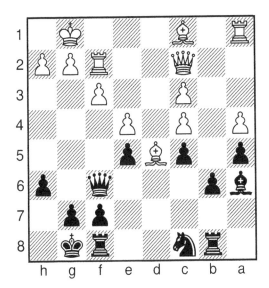

In a 2001 event at the Marshall Chess Club, I had Black here against expert Tony Greco (rated 2018 at the time). Find three candidate moves for Black and decide which is the best one.

Discussion

On my last move I had played 17...♞c8 (from e7) to redeploy it to d6 where (along with my bishop on a6) it will attack White's c4-pawn. So in my mind, I was planning to play ...♞d6 on the very next move since this was a "two-move plan." That is the right destination for the knight, but timing is everything. After 18...♞d6, White gains a dangerous initiative with 19.f4, opening the f-file for his major pieces. Black will need a high degree of defensive accuracy to hold the position.

Instead, 18...g5 *(Restraint)* prevents the f4-pawn's advance, blocking White's kingside attack. The first player still has an advantage, but Black's defensive task is much easier since the battle will now be fought on the queenside where most of Black's pieces are located. From a practical standpoint, it's easier to defend on the queenside in this position than on the kingside.

The lesson here is that when you have a "two-move plan," you must *never* automatically play the second move without first evaluating your opponent's likely response to that second move. No deep calculation is required here. All it takes is freeze-framing the second move in your mind before making it and looking calmly at the board to determine how your opponent is likely to respond. Had I frozen the position in my mind with my knight sitting on d6, it would have been obvious that White's reply would be 19.f4!. My "two-move plan" made White's simple threat invisible to me, especially since his previous move (18.e4) contained no threats and didn't change the position in any significant way.

T101: Black to Move

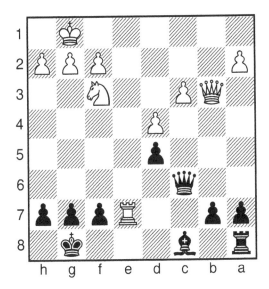

Now that you've completed the 100 training positions in this book, here's a final Bonus position! This is from the game Kritz – Macieja at the 2005 European Championship. Find three candidate moves for Black and choose the best one.

Discussion

Black appears to be in big trouble here because White has very active pieces while Black's bishop and rook are still sitting on their original squares. If you sensed that this is an *Only Move* position, you're right! By now you know the drill for handling "only move" positions: You must consider *every* reasonable move in the position. Go ahead and do that now.

At first glance, 21...b6 looks good, with the intention of protecting the b-pawn and getting the bishop out to b7 or a6. However, the simple refutation is 22.♕xd5 since 22...♕xd5 23.♖e8 is mate! If you chose 21... b6, you missed that simple tactic. Recall that the second step after finding every reasonable candidate move is to visualize (i.e., freeze-frame) the position that will occur on the board after you make each candidate move and determine what your opponent's reply is likely to be. When we're facing life-or-death in an "only move" situation, there are no shortcuts, we simply *must* do the mental work involved in these two steps.

What about 21...♗e6, sacrificing the b7-pawn but finally getting our pieces out? A reasonable choice, since after 22.♖xb7 White is much better but Black is still fighting.

Is 21...♗d7 also a reasonable choice? Yes, but only if you saw the moves 22.♘e5 ♕h6 (saving the bishop due to the threat of mate on c1). However, then the simple 23.♕b2 (or 23.♕d1) retains White's large advantage.

Next in line is 21...f6. Did you choose that move? If so, you have the potential to become a defensive genius – this move gives Black full equality! To gain the maximum value from this training position, explain why Black is equal here. The answer is that 21...f6 shuts the f3-knight out of play and buys time for Black to get his bishop and rook into the game. The game continued 22.♘e1 b6 23.c4! (a very tricky and dangerous move). What would you play now? There are several good moves. Only the two captures (23... dxc4 or 23...♕xc4) are bad for Black, due to 24.♕g3! with a strong attack.

It's fitting that we end this book on defensive methods with a humble pawn move that neutralizes the opponent's whole army! Defense is sometimes exciting, but most of the time it boils down to hanging tough by managing our emotions and applying the types of structured thinking techniques explained in this book. If you have put in the hard work on these 101 positions, you've significantly increased your ability to defend successfully when under pressure!

Index of Key Methods
And Techniques

Below is a list of all the methods and techniques covered in this book. Each topic in the list includes the associated training positions to make it easy for you to locate positions for review and additional practice.

For example, if you did not perform as well on the positions that required cautious (P-R-O) defensive solutions as you did on the positions that required active (A-C-T) solutions, I recommend that you wait a month and then return to those P-R-O positions. Repetition is an essential training technique and is the best way to build pattern recognition.

Defensive Methods (P-R-O-A-C-T)

Prevention (P): T14, T22, T28, T40, T62, T68, T71, T101

Restraint (R): T13, T15, T19, T35, T40, T45, T47, T50, T55, T100

Only Move (O): T6, T10, T12, T16, T59, T60, T69, T70, T72, T74, T94

Activity (A): T9, T18, T20, T29, T30, T39, T57, T62, T76, T79, T82, T88

Counter-Attack (C): T1, T5, T7, T8, T11, T25, T27, T33, T38, T39, T58, T80, T82, T88, T92

Transformation (T): T21, T43, T51, T72, T79, T88, T93

Techniques for Thinking and Managing Your Emotions

Hit the "Reset Button": Sit on Your Hands, Take Deep Breaths, and Calmly Find Candidate Moves: T2

"Just Get On With It": T8, T29

15-Second Freeze Frame: T11, T36, T41, T54, T85, T90

Four Main Signs of a Heightened Emotional State: Introduction

When to Play a "Weaker" Move: T3

Positional Blunders: T52, T82

When Visualization Is More Important Than Calculation: T6, T7

The Danger of Passive Moves Against Higher-Rated Players: T9, T17, T18, T25, T29, T30, T31, T37, T47, T76

Handling Pawn Tension: T23, T84

"Allowing" Your Opponent to Win Material: T20, T24, T51, T79

When Defending and Short on Time, Seek Mobility and Centralization: T26, T76

How to Respond to "Shocking" Moves: T32, T42

Avoid "Redundant" Pieces: T49, T61, T64,

"Loading the Gun": T53, T87

Go "Backward" to Go Forward: T48, T64

Don't Accelerate Your Opponent's Pawn Storm: T46, T65, T73

Beware of the Two-Move Plan: T2, T45, T99

Beware of Triggering Multiple Pawn Exchanges: T52

Don't Hang Onto a Pawn that Must Be Let Go: T77

Acknowledgements

Former World Champion Mikhail Botvinnik once said that the best way to improve your playing strength is to study your own games deeply, especially your losses. So my initial motivation for writing this book was to take his advice to heart. The attentive reader will have noticed that in more than half of the training positions in this book, I did not find the best move.

Among the living, I'd like to thank the guys at Forward Chess, who were enthusiastic about my idea for this book when it was a draft of only a few pages. They put me in touch with Leonid (publisher) and Jorge (editor) at Mongoose Press. Throughout the process, Leonid and Jorge have provided detailed and thoughtful answers to my numerous questions and have collaborated with me on decisions large and small every step of the way!

This book is dedicated to my wife Renee.